STANDARDS
OF PHOTOPLAY
APPRECIATION

A Photoplay Approach to
SHAKESPEARE

STANDARDS

OF PHOTOPLAY

APPRECIATION

Including
A Photoplay Approach to
SHAKESPEARE

WILLIAM LEWIN
*Formerly Chairman, English Department,
Weequahic High School, Newark, New Jersey*

ALEXANDER FRAZIER
*Assistant Superintendent in Charge
of Instruction, Houston, Texas, Public Schools*

EDUCATIONAL & RECREATIONAL GUIDES, INC.
10 BRAINERD ROAD
SUMMIT, NEW JERSEY
1957

Copyright 1953, 1954, 1955, 1956, 1957,

by EDUCATIONAL & RECREATIONAL GUIDES, INC.

Printed in U. S. A.

All rights reserved.

AMERICAN BOOK—STRATFORD PRESS, INC., NEW YORK

Foreword

THIS IS A general introduction to photoplay appreciation. Although it is primarily a textbook for junior and senior high schools, it will be useful also in teacher-training institutions and colleges. It is designed to raise standards of discrimination in the selection of movie entertainment.

The text is an outgrowth of pioneer curriculum units prepared by William Lewin for the National Council of Teachers of English and tested throughout the nation in a controlled experiment conducted a generation ago. The findings were reported in the Council's Monograph No. 2, *Photoplay Appreciation in American High Schools,* published by Appleton-Century in 1934. The publication of the present text is, in a sense, a continuation of the original effort of the NCTE to raise movie standards. It is hoped that the new text will help to educate the rising generation to demand better movie fare.

During the past 22 years, the discussion of movies has gradually become an established part of the curriculum of American high schools. Many high schools now show 16mm versions of theatrical features during or after school hours as a phase of the audio-visual program. Some elementary schools show features in their auditoriums as a phase of training in audience behavior and in proper use of leisure time. Schools cooperate with theatres to build better movie habits.

To stimulate the upward trend in the photoplay-appreciation movement, Dr. Lewin has published since 1929 some 250 guides to the discussion of photoplays, with a total circulation of about 10,000,000 copies. These constitute a periodical called *Photoplay Studies.* They serve as current supplements to this basic text, as do the filmstrips listed on page 160.

By means of the text, in combination with the issues of *Photoplay Studies,* we can give more serious attention to one of the most important findings reported in the Lewin Monograph—*that it is futile to expect any significant improvement in young people's movie tastes unless the teaching procedure includes a series of at least fourteen class periods* devoted to the discussion of a minimum of seven selected pictures—two 40-minute periods to each discussion. The pioneer report recommended that the curriculum unit in photoplay appreciation, to be fully effective, should comprise ten 2-period discussions, following closely after seeing the photoplay.

One of the practical problems confronting the teacher who wishes to secure full participation in a photoplay discussion has been the lack of school facilities to show feature films. Teachers have until recently been content to let those who have seen recommended films in theaters arrange panel discussions. Now, convenient 16mm projectors have been developed for auditoriums. Schools today may therefore do a much better job of utilizing children's natural interest in movies.

Contents

1. Why Study Photoplay Appreciation? 1
2. Where Did the Movies Come From? 5
3. Who Makes the Movies? 20
4. Standards of Photoplay Production 28
5. Standards of Story Material 34
6. Notable Screen Writers 39
7. Standards of Direction 44
8. Notable Photoplay Directors 51
9. Standards of Photoplay Acting 63
10. Notable Screen Actors 69
11. Standards of Cinematography 83
12. Notable Cinematographers 88
13. Standards of Photoplay Editing 93
14. What Makes a Photoplay Significant? 102
15. How to Become a Better Movie-Goer 108
16. What Shall We Read About the Movies? . . . 116
17. Glossary of Motion-Picture Terms 119
18. A Photoplay Approach to Shakespeare . . . 122

1

Why Study Photoplay Appreciation?

How many movies are truly memorable? How many refresh you, stimulate you, lift up your heart, make you laugh or weep, thrill you with a sense of beauty?

From a photoplay have you a right to expect something that will add to your understanding of life and your ability to face it? Or don't you care?

Every time you buy a ticket at your neighborhood theater, nevertheless, you cast a vote for the particular picture you patronize. By your attendance you indicate what type of picture you want made. Thus you reveal your taste in movies.

As you grow from childhood to adulthood, your tastes change. Some people's tastes change more rapidly than those of others. But all tastes change. We learn to like what at first we did not like. This is because we come to appreciate, through knowledge and experience, what we previously could not understand or enjoy.

Fortunate indeed are those who gradually learn that one of the exciting adventures in life is to explore what art, music, literature, science, and philosophy offer us. This adventure in critical exploration may be applied to movie-going. What photoplays reach high standards of truth and beauty? Which are merely forms of amusement, of little significance?

The purpose of these chapters is to help you develop independent judgment regarding the many types of movies you see. Here you will find standards for appreciating photoplays. By studying the information given in the following pages, you will learn to "shop" for the best movies.

To get your money's worth in movies, you must consider more than what appears on the marquee of a theater. You must learn to evaluate what advertisements say about pictures. You must learn the names of the best producers, directors, and writers. Not all movies present life-problems that are real, characterizations that are lifelike, plots that are logical, endings that are natural, performances that are convincing.

By improving your own taste in movies, you help to raise the general level of public taste. In this way you stimulate the production of better movies. If better movies are to come, it must be because the public is more intelligent and discriminating in patronizing entertainment. For it is true today, as it was centuries ago, that "the stage but echoes back the public voice." Those engaged in play-making must please audiences if they are to succeed. "The drama's laws the drama's patrons give" is an axiom of show business. A movie studio must please great masses of people or go out of business.

Showmanship, indeed, may be defined as the art of pleasing the greatest possible number of people. Unless the movie producer can please a sufficiently large public, he cannot recapture the large investment which his picture represents. His job is to earn profits for his company by appealing to the masses. A publisher may bring out a novel, a biography, a book of poems, or a textbook for a few thousand dollars. Even the producer of a stage-play risks only moderate sums. The producer of a photoplay, however, needs very large sums. He cannot afford to invest millions of dollars in artistic photoplays that may not win wide support. Only if the public will support films with great themes will those who plan our movies make subjects with such themes.

Creative workers at picture studios sometimes sigh over the poor taste of people who go in large numbers to see unworthy movies. But movie-makers must follow the law of supply and demand. The risk of making artistic pictures which the public may fail to support is too great for those who hold the purse-strings of production.

Thus it is that worried producers tend to fall back on trite formulas when they find that "horse operas," "soap operas," back-stage musicals, and routine boy-meets-girl movies are less risky than original ideas. Is the cut-and-dried movie "as you like it"—one in which you can easily forecast that the hero will defeat the villain? Or that the cop will capture the criminal? Or that the boy will first lose and then win the girl? By carelessly patronizing such movies rather than carefully "shopping" for truly fine photoplays you may be failing to get a full measure of entertainment value for the time and money you spend in theaters.

To help stimulate the production of better pictures choose your movies as wisely as you can. By patronizing the truly outstanding photoplays, you can do your part toward increasing the number of such productions. This book will help you improve your ability as an entertainment-shopper and increase your ability to participate in intelligent movie discussion.

Suggested Activities

1. Obtain at your library a list of the "ten best" movies in a recent poll, such as the *Film Daily's* annual poll of the nation's movie critics. How many of these movies did you see?

4 • Standards of Photoplay Appreciation

How would you rate yourself as a movie-shopper? Do you consider yourself a discriminating movie-goer?

2. Write your autobiography as a movie-goer (or prepare to talk on this topic). When did you see your first motion picture? What do you consider the best films you have ever seen? How have your tastes in motion pictures changed since your earliest days of movie-going?

3. As a class project, reserve a section of your bulletin board for posting clippings of critical reviews of the new motion pictures. Ask your library for magazines that publish regular film reviews. A committee might assume responsibility for keeping the bulletin board "movie corner" up to date.

2

Where Did the Movies Come From?

THE MOVIES had humble beginnings. In the spring of 1896, the first commercial showing of motion pictures in the United States occurred in a New York music hall, near where Macy's department store now stands. Coming at the end of a vaudeville program, the movies were a series of one-minute scenes of a variety of persons and things. Some of the titles were *Sea Waves, A Boxing Bout, Venice Showing Gondolas, Butterfly Dance,* and *Kaiser Wilhelm Reviewing His Troops.*

What these 50-foot scenes had in common was that they showed action. They were *moving* pictures. Perhaps the audience was more mystified than entertained by pictures that could move. The movement of the characters was so jerky and the projection so poor that the movies were called "flickers." In the early days following their introduction, motion pictures were also spoken of as "chasers" when shown on the same program with acts by living performers. They were used to signify the end of the program and to clear the theater for a new audience.

Twenty years later, in 1915, Los Angeles witnessed the première of the first truly significant American motion picture, *The Birth of a Nation,* directed by D. W. Griffith. Based on *The Clansman,* a popular novel and play by Thomas Dixon, the film told a story of Reconstruction days in the South, playing up the role of the Ku-Klux Klan. Praised everywhere for its magnificent power as story-telling, *The Birth of a Nation* was nevertheless attacked for its anti-Negro bias by such leaders as Jane Addams, Chicago social welfare pioneer, and Charles W. Eliot, president of Harvard University. Yet millions went to see it. *The Birth of a Nation* was roadshown in towns and villages that had no regular moviehouses. It was a great money-maker. Today it is still studied, not for what it has to say, but for the techniques of story-telling used by its director.

Thus in twenty years the movies had come of age. Between the first "flickers" and the masterpieces made by Griffith lies the story of how a great new industry was built.

Inventors and investors played a big part in this development, not only in the United States, but also in England and France. Thomas A. Edison led the way with the peep-show Kinetoscope, a machine that was soon very popular with penny-arcade customers. It remains in use even today. Edison felt that since only one person at a time could see moving pictures in the peep-show, the "novelty" would last longer and be more profitable. He realized later that he had a medium of continuing mass appeal. A machine that could throw the pictures on a screen, so that large audiences could witness them, was needed. Such a machine was soon developed, and similar projectors were designed abroad.

At first the novelty of the movies had made them popular with the vaudeville houses. In 1902 what may have been the first all-movie theater was opened in Los Angeles. Advertising "Up-to-Date, High-Class Motion-Picture Entertainment, Especially for Women and Children," the Electric Theater charged five cents admission. It was an immediate success.

News of the money to be made by showing full programs of movies in separate movie-houses spread. Store buildings and former penny-arcades were reopened as movie theaters. Three years later a theater showing films with piano accompaniment was opened in Pittsburgh. The name it bore, the Nickelodeon, became a synonym for the motion-picture theater. So rapid was the growth of the movie audience that in 1914 New York witnessed the opening of the first of the million-dollar "movie palaces." One of these, Warner's Strand Theater, seated 3,000 persons. In twenty years, the great audience and its theaters had been built.

Most important of all in this development, of course, was the rapid improvement of the quality of film production. The first movies, made with direct sunlight because Edison's electric lamp was as yet insufficiently developed, had been merely pictures of motion. For the peep-shows, this motion had sometimes been found chiefly in dancers and comedy gags. For "chasers," almost any motion would do. Trains, crowds, parades, fire engines, waterfalls, and street scenes were frequently shown. News events, such as President McKinley's inauguration and Queen Victoria's funeral, were also filmed. But the camera was immobile. It was set in one place and it photographed whatever came before it.

In those early years, story quality was hardly considered. The brief movies might show a single situation, comic (a man sneezing) or pathetic (a dog at his master's grave), but the accepted limit of one or two minutes made artistic story-telling impossible.

It was not until the importation of several motion pictures produced by a Frenchman, George Melies, that story-telling on the screen began. In 1900, Melies produced *Cinderella*, a seven-minute story-film with "artificially arranged" scenes, settings, costumes, and trick photography. An American,

Edwin S. Porter, studied the tricks of Melies and became the first important American director.

Porter saw in the principle of planning and photographing a series of scenes the essence of story-telling. Working for the Edison studios at the time, he had made shots of fire engines

This replica model of the "Black Maria," the world's first motion-picture studio, is now open to the public at the Edison Museum, West Orange, New Jersey. The original was built in 1892 by Thomas A. Edison, the great inventor and founder of the motion picture industry. Photo, courtesy of Thomas A. Edison Foundation Museum, West Orange, New Jersey.

on the run, of ladders being placed against buildings, and of fire-fighting. Although made at different times, they all dealt with the same theme. It occurred to Porter that by piecing these scenes together and adding new ones to provide a little

Where Did the Movies Come From? • 9

The administration building of the Metro-Goldwyn-Mayer studios at Culver City, California.

Aerial view of the Metro-Goldwyn-Mayer studios at Culver City, California.

plot, he might have a story-film. He created scenes of rescue and, by interweaving these with existing scenes, produced in 1902 the first American story-film, *The Life of an American Fireman*. Porter had made a great discovery—that film scenes could be assembled and edited to tell a story. He went beyond

Melies, whose scenes were all photographed in one continuous sequence. Porter was the first to do what today all studios do —build up photoplays of shots put together like the pieces of a mosaic. Portions of scenes, shot at various times and places, are assembled bit by bit. Thus was established the principle of editing or cutting in movie-making.

The next year Porter made *The Great Train Robbery* along the Lackawanna Railroad near Paterson, New Jersey. This crude film is of historical importance because it was the forerunner of our popular westerns. It set the pattern for the outdoor-action type of film destined to be made in greater numbers than any other type.

The early story-films were still short, running eight to ten minutes. The action was quick and obvious. There was no time to be subtle. Characters had to be immediately recognizable as good or bad. Gestures and facial reactions were such as could be picked up by a fixed camera, always kept in the same place. It remained for Griffith to achieve camera mobility and to discover the use of the close-up. Porter had indeed used one as a tailpiece at the end of *The Great Train Robbery*. A robber fired his pistol directly at the audience, but the shot had no connection with the story.

When Griffith went to work as a director in 1908, he was ashamed to have his real name appear on the screen. His ambition had been to write poems and plays. He thought, as did many other persons connected with the theater, that working in the movies was rather disgraceful. Yet he was the first of the directors to see the camera as the true story-teller. In the first years of his experience, he carried the art of movie-making into unexplored fields. He was truly a creative artist.

Melies had shown Porter how to break up a story into scenes. Porter showed Griffith how to piece scenes together with variety and contrast, without having to take all scenes on the same roll of film. Griffith was to show others how to take each scene and break it up into shots at various angles. Instead of treating the scene as if it had to be photographed from the same spot during its entirety, Griffith began to move the camera from one place to another. He was the first to move the camera so as to catch the most important action of a scene and leave out other action for the moment. He learned the effectiveness of drawing far back from the scene, particularly in outdoor pictures, to give a feeling of the sweep and beauty of the landscape, and of using the close-up for emphasis. From these shots, he would then edit the scene, putting the various pieces together to form a unit.

This technique of varying the camera angle is so familiar today that one is not usually aware of how many different shots are combined to make each scene. Yet as Griffith began to develop his way of working, he was considered to be trying for the impossible. One of his ideas was to vary the amount of light on the scene so as to create mood and atmosphere. He kept trying new ideas. The test always came in the reactions of audiences. They liked his films. He became the most popular of directors. His techniques were admired and widely copied.

Griffith carried further Porter's idea of alternating scenes from different story threads. Sometimes he used this device for contrast. By means of rapid alternation of scenes of parallel action, he built suspense in numerous chases and rescues. Cross-cutting, back and forth, from the pursuing posse to the fleeing villain, he built up audience tension. Griffith's device is now familiar to all lovers of outdoor-action melodramas.

Griffith's freeing the camera of its fixed position resulted in a more natural style of acting. This was possible because the camera, by coming close, could emphasize the smallest hint of expression. Ranting and raving were no longer necessary. The camera instead of the actor created the effect sought by the director.

Another important director, Mack Sennett, discovered that by turning the camera more slowly than usual, he could make the action on the screen appear faster. Thus in his slapstick comedies he secured the effect of a great bustling around. Sennett specialized in the farcical chase. His Keystone Cops made movie history. He introduced the custard pie as a comic weapon. Charlie Chaplin got his start in the Sennett studios.

Thomas Ince was still another important pioneer director. He was the first to organize a businesslike procedure for filming several pictures at the same time. He was the first great movie supervisor. He centered his talent on developing strong stories and turning them over to other directors. When the scenes had been shot, he closely supervised the cutting and editing. The westerns starring William S. Hart, which Ince produced, set the pattern for the most popular type of story the screen has known.

The Star System

In addition to the enterprise of inventors and investors in perfecting and promoting the movies and the ingenuity of pioneer directors in learning how to tell an exciting story through the new medium, the star system contributed to the rapid rise of American movies as popular entertainment. At first, companies kept the names of favored actors and actresses to themselves. But in 1910 picture companies began to issue magazines with pictures and stories about their featured players, thus starting the "fan" magazines.

Many of the early stars have long been forgotten. The two greatest were Mary Pickford and Charles Chaplin. "Little Mary" achieved the most remarkable success of any of the early stars. The roles selected for her were mostly in Cinderella stories, such as *Poor Little Rich Girl, Little Princess, Such a Little Queen, Little Pal,* and *Rebecca of Sunnybrook Farm.* The public eagerly welcomed these "pollyanodynes," emphasizing the belief that life will reward sweetness and virtue and that "all's right with the world."

Regarded by many critics as one of the greatest geniuses of the screen, Charlie Chaplin rose rapidly as a master of pantomime. Portraying a tramp with baggy pants, floppy shoes, old derby hat, and little mustache, he carried a cane which became the symbol of his comic aspirations to be a gentleman. The public found the pathetic little tramp's adventures in *The Count, The Floorwalker,* and *The Immigrant* touching and hilarious at the same time.

The star system has developed many big names. Moviegoers are often better acquainted with the private lives of movie stars than with the affairs of close relatives. The screen gives its audience intimate insight into the personalities of stars. Each star is the center of a huge publicity machine that constantly sends out columns of news and gossip. Stars have become household figures to the American public. Theaters feature on their marquees, above all, the names of stars.

Among the early women movie stars following Mary Pickford were Theda Bara, Pearl White, and Lillian Gish. Theda Bara's appearance in *A Fool There Was* (1915) introduced the "vamp," or *la femme fatale,* the woman who lured men to destruction. Among those who succeeded her as "the woman with a past" are Pola Negri, Greta Garbo, Marlene Dietrich, and Ava Gardner. Pearl White was famous in her day as the "serial queen." Her most notable serial was *The Perils of Pauline* (1920).

D. W. Griffith's favorite actress was Lillian Gish. Following her stardom in *The Birth of a Nation* and *Intolerance,* her delicate and wistful appearance continued to appeal to the public in Griffith's *Broken Blossoms* (1919) and *Orphans of the Storm* (1922).

Male movie stars of note in this early period included Rudolph Valentino, Douglas Fairbanks, and Richard Barthelmess. Perhaps no romantic actor of silent days enjoyed greater popularity than Valentino. *The Shiek* (1920), *Blood and Sand* (1920), and *The Four Horsemen of the Apocalypse* (1921) placed him at the head of the list. His appearance assured the success of almost any film.

Another romantic figure, Douglas Fairbanks, Senior, was a natural athlete and acrobat. He was a lively hero in such films as *Robin Hood* (1922), *The Thief of Bagdad* (1924), and *The Black Pirate* (1926). Richard Barthelmess established his stardom in *Tol'able David* (1921). He co-starred with Lillian Gish in *Broken Blossoms* and *Way Down East*.

In these early days, Chaplin continued to make movie history with *The Kid* (1920), *The Gold Rush* (1925), and *The Circus* (1928).

So it was that within twenty or twenty-five years after their humble beginnings, motion pictures in America had become a great entertainment business. Edison and others had solved the problem of inventing or perfecting the needed machines and equipment. With their characteristic quickness to sense new markets, American businessmen had built the theaters and sold the pictures to the waiting millions. Directors like Griffith, Porter, and Ince had created the craft that was required for mastery of the new medium. The star system had added a personal touch to the motion-picture industry.

Following World War I, the movies quickly came into their own as a form of communication that could no longer be ignored by the serious critic of American life. The stepped-up development of the movies was influenced by many factors, not the least of which were the example of foreign-made films and the advent of the talking motion picture.

European Photoplays

Americans, while they have maintained world leadership in the motion-picture industry, have always profited from studying the product of foreign film-makers, beginning with Melies and his *Cinderella* and continuing all the way down to today's interest in Italian movies.

In 1913 an Italian-made movie version of *Quo Vadis* was imported and shown in a first-class Broadway theater at advanced admission prices. Packing the theater daily for six months, it proved that a spectacle running for two and a half hours would appeal to masses of people. Roadshown throughout the country, this foreign-made film proved so popular that the feature-length film was immediately established as profitable. It paved the way for Griffith to make *The Birth of a Nation* in 1915.

During World War I, while movie studios in Europe were forced to close, American movies continued to develop rapidly. With production abroad at a standstill, the Hollywood studios began to dominate the world market. However, soon after the war ended, the studios of Germany, Russia, and Sweden began to turn out pictures that greatly influenced American movies.

A German film, *The Cabinet of Dr. Caligari* (1919), told the imaginative story of a madman in scenes as they appeared to the distorted mind of the madman himself. The camera for the first time looked back into a man's mind. Full of fantastic sequences, the film was hailed as a great work of cinematic art. While not a popular success, it was widely studied by the makers of movies in this and other countries. It is shown from time to time at the Museum of Modern Art in New York as one of its series to illustrate movie history.

Two ace German directors, Ernst Lubitsch and F. W. Murnau, came to Hollywood. Lubitsch, who had made spectacular movies in Germany, now made intimate, satirical, and sophisticated comedies, such as *The Marriage Circle* (1924). He became famous for deft touches that emphasized significant details in lightning-like flashes, for daring camera shots from unusual angles, for effective lighting, and for charming cinematic rhythm. When sound came, he made brilliant and witty use of music to enhance action and dialog. His comedy, *The Love Parade* (1929), with Jeanette MacDonald and Maurice Chevalier, was highly successful.

F. W. Murnau had made *The Last Laugh* (1921) in Germany, with the great actor, Emil Jannings, telling his story almost entirely in pantomime. His best American picture was *Sunrise* (1927).

The Russian school of directors, studying Griffith's work, developed the film for Communist purposes. They have used the photoplay powerfully to influence the thinking of masses of peasants. In Russia, the motion picture thus became primarily propaganda. The purpose of the studios, all government-owned, has been to use the new medium to sway the feelings of hundreds of millions of people toward communism and against capitalism. Chief exponent of the propaganda technique, following the Communist Revolution of 1917, was Sergei Eisenstein. His best-known works were *The Battleship Potemkin* (1925), *Ten Days That Shook the World* (1927), and *October* (1928). Scorning the use of professional actors, Eisenstein made the camera the actor; he felt that it could tell the story alone. One of the significant Russian cinematic devices was to take shots of different objects, or of the hands, feet, and faces of different persons, and then combine these by careful editing to form a sequence or "montage" which produced a desired effect. The "montage" has become established as a part of modern film technique.

American motion pictures profited from the study given by their directors to the best work of foreign directors, just as the films of the Germans, French, and Russians had become better when they studied the work of D. W. Griffith.

Sound Comes to the Screen

When sound came to the screen, however, much that had once been mastered had to be restudied. A new dimension was added, but the universal appeal of the silent picture was diminished. New techniques had to be invented to deal with new problems.

The screen found its voice in 1927. In *The Jazz Singer,* Al Jolson, the "greatest mammy singer of them all," electrified Broadway in his screen debut. Warner Brothers achieved one of the greatest "firsts" in movie history by successfully presenting Jolson in the first feature film with dialog. Theater managers everywhere demanded sound films. The studios responded. Within three years the motion-picture industry paid hundreds of millions of dollars to Western Electric Company and to Radio Corporation of America to install sound equipment. The revolution was complete.

With the coming of sound, many great silent stars were destined to fall. Their voices did not record well or were inappropriate to their visual personalities. Moreover, the spoken word made it possible to convey many subtle shades of meaning that left less to be said by the actor through face and gesture. Some of the older stars were not able to adapt themselves to the more reserved or quiet kind of acting required in sound films. Their techniques remained the same as those that had ensured them popularity and stardom a few years back, but they seemed to be overacting all the time. New faces and new voices soon replaced many stars who flourished before 1927.

By 1930, the motion picture had become the most popular form of entertainment in America. Every week, millions of movie-goers flocked to the theaters to see the newest releases from Hollywood, the film capital of the world. The influence of the movies began to be felt in many phases of our national life—in new slang phrases, in dress styles, in home decoration, in manners, and, some critics felt, in morals.

Because motion pictures are important in the lives of so many people they are now taken much more seriously than they used to be. Many good books have been written on the movies. Schools are including the study of films in their curricula. In towns and cities across the country, groups of men and women who think that films are important are banded together to study old films and new ones. Inevitably, the growth of color television broadcasting is destined to make the study and discussion of photoplays more important than ever before.

In this book, an attempt is made to provide students of the movies with a background that will add to their enjoyment of movie-going by increasing their understanding of what goes to make up a superior motion picture.

Suggested Activities

1. Interview several older persons in your neighborhood about their memories of the early days of motion pictures. What stars do they remember? If they recall any of the motion pictures discussed in this chapter, what do they have to say about them?

2. Select one of the movie stars or directors of earlier days

to look up in books available to you in your school or public library. See what you can find about early movies in bound volumes of magazines of the past fifty years.

3. Make a list of important dates, events, and names from the early history of the motion picture as set forth in this chapter. Add to the list from other reading that you may do.

4. Begin to build a vocabulary of terms that will be helpful in discussing motion pictures and their development as a force in American life: *Kinetoscope, Nickelodeon,* etc.

5. Compare the present status of television with that of the movies in their early days. Can you note any similarities?

3

Who Makes the Movies?

Some critics of motion pictures have questioned whether making films is an art. "How can the product of dozens or even hundreds of persons be called an art?" they have asked. "Art comes as an expression of the feeling and knowledge of a single person. It is given form and meaning by the intensity and integrity of his individuality."

Movie critics may be willing, as occasionally they are, to grant that a movie-maker who assumes total responsibility for a film may approach the status of an artist. But for the ordinary film, they see little chance of anyone's taking it seriously —at least, as art.

Yet there are others, including teachers, who hold that movie-making at its best is truly an art. They grant that movie art depends on the cooperation of many artists and craftsmen —writers, actors, directors, set designers, photographers, musicians, recording engineers, and editors. They grant, too, that great art is not found so often in films as one might like. And when a motion picture is great, they will say, there is always a single artist who dominates and coordinates every detail of production—as David O. Selznick did in making *Gone With the Wind*. The producer or director, or the producer-director, is that person. Through the singleness of vision of one person, working with many others, the film can be and sometimes is a work of art.

Whichever viewpoint we may tend to accept about the film as art, there is one strange fact about the making of motion pictures that we can all agree upon. The names of most of the outstanding persons working in the movies are unknown to us except for the actors and actresses. How many producers, directors, scenario-writers, composers, cameramen, or set designers do you know by name? You might check yourself at this point. Look at the following list. How many can you identify according to their work?

1. Alfred Hitchcock
2. Joseph L. Mankiewicz
3. Jack Cardiff
4. John Ford
5. Dore Schary
6. Cedric Gibbons
7. James Wong Howe
8. John Huston
9. Arthur Freed
10. Alfred Newman
11. Frank Nugent
12. Philip Dunne
13. Hans Dreier
14. Jean Renoir
15. Dmitri Tiomkin
16. René Clair
17. Victor Young
18. Darryl Zanuck

Some of these names are doubtless familiar to you by sight. You have seen them in the lists of "screen credits" that follow the main title of the photoplay. It should help you to become a better movie-goer if you learn more about the work of these people. What they do is even more important than the work of actors and actresses.

In Chapter 2 we spoke of Thomas Ince as the first person to lay down the pattern of the movie director-general on a

NOTE: Key to the identity of the eighteen names: Producers: 5, 9, 18. Directors: 1, 2, 4, 8, 14, 16. Writers: 11, 12. Musical composers and directors: 10, 15, 17. Cameramen: 3, 7. Art directors: 6, 13.

large scale. He planned the films that were to be made by his studio, working with writers to turn out complete scripts that could then be turned over to other directors to be filmed as written. Today such supervisors are known as producers. Their responsibilities are very great.

Let us look at the way the producer works in a large film company, such as Metro-Goldwyn-Mayer or 20th Century-Fox. He is one of a number of producers working for his company. From the reading department that synopsizes and recommends new novels, short stories, plays, biographies, and original stories written directly for the screen, he may be given a number to consider for filming. Perhaps he has read many synopses and found a story he likes. It is probably one of the kind that he has handled successfully before.

With the story, he goes to writers on the staff of his studio to begin the long process of working out a complete scenario for the filming of the movie. He may work with several writers before he is satisfied with the final result. Meanwhile he is selecting one of the company's directors to take over the major responsibility of translating the story into pictures. Sometimes the director will sit in with the producer and the writer to contribute his ideas. The producer then has the responsibilty of selecting a cast to enact the story, or he may have had one or more stars in mind from the start. He selects actors from those under contract to his company and may also seek permission to borrow available actors from other companies. By this time he has begun conferring with the art and wardrobe directors on problems of preparing sets and costumes. It may be that he now needs to call upon the research department to be sure that everything is correct. He must also choose a cameraman to work with his director.

Now the time has come to begin photographing the scenes. The producer, who may be starting work at this point on another picture, keeps in touch with the progress being made. He sees to it that the publicity department sends out news stories on the new production. He views scenes from the new film as they are completed. He may suggest the need for additional dialog or changes in the script. In short, after planning the film, he supervises its making and is held responsible for its success or failure. It is the producer who coordinates the work of the many artists and craftsmen whose efforts must be harmonized and controlled for the sake of the final screen result.

Who are some of the important producers of motion pictures? One is Darryl Zanuck, for many years executive head of the 20th Century-Fox studio, who has to his credit many fine pictures made under his supervision, including *The Grapes of Wrath* (1940), *The Ox Bow Incident* (1943), *Wilson* (1944), *Gentleman's Agreement* (1947), *The Snake Pit* (1948), *Pinky* (1949), *Twelve O'Clock High* (1950), and a procession of CinemaScope films, beginning with *The Robe* (1953).

Another is David O. Selznick, responsible for one of the most ambitious pictures ever made, *Gone With the Wind* (1939). Selznick spent two years planning the picture and two years making it, at a cost of $3,850,000. The film as released ran for three hours and forty minutes. It was released in 1954 for the fifth time and has become a film classic. Other Selznick productions include *David Copperfield* (1935), *Rebecca* (1940), and *The Fallen Idol* (1949).

Perhaps the best-known producer is Samuel Goldwyn, one of the pioneers of the film industry. He was one of the men who formed the company that later merged with others to become Metro-Goldwyn-Mayer. Samuel Goldwyn is not connected with M-G-M; he has been an independent producer of films since 1923.

One of Goldwyn's strengths lies in his selection of stories, as shown in such successes as *Arrowsmith* (1931), *Dodsworth* (1936), *Dead End* (1937), *Wuthering Heights* (1939), *The Little Foxes* (1941), *The Best Years of Our Lives* (1946), and *Guys and Dolls* (1956). He is noted for working persistently to get a picture just right. As a result, *The Best Years of Our Lives* received nine of the Motion Picture Academy Awards for 1946.

Another outstanding producer is Walt Disney. Coordinating the work of hundreds of creative artists and extraordinarily clever craftsmen, he turns out one success after another. His first animated cartoon, *Plane Crazy,* appeared in 1928 and introduced Mickey Mouse. A year later, he produced *The Skeleton Dance,* another short subject, but one which used classical music as a background. The success of his cartoons was largely responsible for driving off the screen the formerly popular two-reel comedies. Soon the cartoon became a standard part of the program of almost every theater, along with the newsreel and feature. One of his most popular earlier short cartoons was entitled *Three Little Pigs* (1933). Its song, "Who's Afraid of the Big Bad Wolf," became a popular hit, expressing the kind of courage needed in those depression days.

When *Snow White and the Seven Dwarfs* appeared in 1938 as the first feature-length cartoon, Disney entered a new phase of production. Since then, he has turned out a dozen such features, including *Pinocchio* (1940), *Fantasia* (1940), *Bambi* (1942), *Song of the South* (1946), *Adventures of Ichabod and Mr. Toad* (1949), and *Cinderella* (1950). More recently he has made a number of live-action photoplays, including *Robin Hood* (1952), and some remarkable shorts on nature study, called *True Life Adventures.*

Five other producers may be mentioned briefly. Jesse L.

Lasky, another pioneer, has had a distinguished career. One of his successes was *Sergeant York* (1941). Irving Thalberg died just before his greatest production, *The Good Earth* (1937), appeared. That picture, a triumph of research and preparation, required nearly a year to film, following three years of planning. Sydney Box is an English producer, notable for such films as *The Seventh Veil* (1945) and *Quartet* (1949). Arthur Freed of M-G-M set new standards of creative production in the dance and musical-comedy field in 1951 with the award-winning *An American in Paris,* voted by the Academy of Motion Picture Arts and Sciences the best picture of the year. Freed himself received the Thalberg Award for consistent top-notch production.

Joseph Pasternak is another specialist in musical productions. He was responsible for the early Deanna Durbin films and more recently for *Holiday in Mexico* (1946), *In the Good Old Summertime* (1949), *Skirts Ahoy* (1952), and *The Student Prince* (1954). Louis de Rochemont, for years the producer of the March of Time series of news reports, has become noted for his realistic productions of semi-documentary films, partly based on fact, such as *The House on 92nd Street* (1945), *Boomerang* (1947), *Lost Boundaries* (1949), and *Walk East on Beacon* (1952).

Our twentieth century has become the age of big business. Motion picture production has inevitably become big business—a great industry. Many small firms have grown and merged with other firms to make gigantic corporations. Since the days when Jesse Lasky and Cecil DeMille began making pictures in a Hollywood barn, the industry has grown until today the largest studios are little cities in themselves, with their own police departments, fire departments, and hospitals. The magnificent M-G-M producing organization employs three thousand technical and creative workers. In California there are now eight major producing organizations. The largest of these are Metro, 20th Century-Fox, Paramount, and Warner Brothers. Next in rank are Universal-International, Columbia, RKO, and Republic. The rise of independent companies is exemplified in Hecht-Lancaster, whose *Marty* won the 1955 Academy Award as the best picture of the year.

Movie production is a keenly competitive business. Its standards are consequently high. Each major studio has its roster of stars, directors, writers, cameramen, costume designers, artists, architects, make-up experts—and executive producers. The responsibility of the producer for the success of a motion picture becomes very great as he selects members of the production team for any given film. His decisions largely determine the quality of the production.

Suggested Activities

1. Examine the publicity and advertising of current motion pictures in your local newspapers. Find out which studios are most frequently mentioned.

2. Write to one of the major studios, explaining that you are a student and need free material for your class about the studio's forthcoming film releases. Analyze the material you receive for an oral report to the class on the type of productions that seem to characterize the studio.

3. Look up the biography of one of the producers discussed in this chapter, using the *Readers' Guide to Periodical Literature* and *Current Biography* to locate information. Prepare a report on the achievements of the producer whom you choose, mentioning an example of his resourcefulness.

For instance, when David O. Selznick was faced with the problem of casting Scarlet O'Hara in *Gone With the Wind,* he turned his stumbling-block into a stepping-stone by dramatizing his wide search. His publicity staff built up suspense in the public mind regarding the casting. As interest mounted throughout the English-speaking world, he screen-tested actress after actress until he found the perfect girl for the part—Vivien Leigh—and launched her on her career as a great star. *Gone With the Wind* made motion-picture history because of the extraordinary resourcefulness of the producer. He won well-deserved financial success and artistic acclaim.

4

Standards of Photoplay Production

WE HAVE LEARNED that behind every photoplay worthy of appreciation lies the plan of an able producer. The work of the producer is extremely complex, for he is concerned with the work of movie-making in all its phases. He must not only select the story to be filmed but must also supervise the preparation of the scenario, the selection of the players, the work of the director, and finally, the editing.

His main interest is necessarily a commercial one. From his standpoint, a good movie is one that does well at the box-office. The probable reactions of audiences in terms of their desire to buy tickets for the film is the decisive factor in all his planning. This is because it costs usually hundreds of thousands of dollars, sometimes millions, to produce a good photoplay.

No matter how enterprising and intelligent a photoplay producer may be, his plan must be based on the most practical considerations. He must follow the trend of current demand for mass entertainment. He must consider the types of films which theater managers everywhere are seeking for their patrons. He must satisfy the needs not only of a national but of a world market. Spectacular films, like *The Greatest Show on Earth* and *Ben Hur,* are in greatest demand. Unless such costly films are made in a manner to please people everywhere, they cannot return a profit. Because of the great investments necessary for making features, the producer tries to purvey pictures of universal appeal.

In doing this the production executive must usually work within the limitations of his studio's roster of players under contract. To borrow stars from other studios is often difficult and expensive. To develop new stars from promising young players, on the other hand, takes time. Nevertheless producers go to a great deal of trouble and expense to secure the best possible casting. For even a minor part they arrange screen tests for a dozen possible players before choosing one.

The producer must take full advantage also of the story properties owned by his studio. The movie rights to copyrighted novels, plays, and other literary materials often command very high prices when they have proved popular. Producers may prefer to revamp stories which their studios already own, to do old things in new ways, rather than go to the expense of securing new story material. Paramount, Metro-Goldwyn-Mayer, 20th Century-Fox, and other large studios have often "played safe" by screening new versions of stories which they have long owned. Paramount remade Theodore Dreiser's *An American Tragedy* in a successful new version called *A Place in the Sun.* Paramount likewise, with artistic and financial success, remade *The Virginian* as *Spawn of the North,* substituting Russian salmon-thieves in Alaskan waters for American cattle-thieves in Wyoming. Metro has long owned the movie rights to Rafael Sabatini's *Scaramouche.* In 1923 it starred Ramon Novarro in a silent version; in 1952 it starred Stewart Granger in a colorful new version. Metro did the same with *Prisoner of Zenda* and is making a new version of *Ben Hur,* which was the studio's first spectacle.

Able producers economize on story costs by using classics on which copyright no longer exists. But the classic must suit current public tastes and must be within the resources of the studio. For example, after making *Quo Vadis,* Metro had a great amount of research material, props, sets, costumes, and production know-how in relation to ancient Rome. Taking advantage of this, the studio made a screen version of Shakespeare's *Julius Caesar.* The Shakespearean production combined universal appeal with a special timeliness rooted in the keen interest of democratic countries in the threat of dictatorships. Dore Schary, production chief at Metro, felt that *Julius Caesar* was "the most excitingly filmable" of Shakespeare's plays. He had in mind the spectacular forum scene in which Antony plays on the fickleness of the Roman mob. Under the spell of rabble-rousing politicians, modern mobs have behaved likewise.

The plans of a producer may at times be severely limited nevertheless by the financial policies of his particular studio and by the budget under which he may be currently operating. The loss of foreign markets, the competition of television, reductions in purchasing power of great masses of people—these are factors which shape financial policies. A producer may be forced to make small comedies and inexpensive outdoor-action melodramas rather than risk losing money on more ambitious productions. He must keep strictly within the bounds set by sound business judgment.

Once a producer decides to make a picture, he must make sure that his plans are as nearly complete as possible before a single scene is shot. His screenplay script must present a clear visualization of every scene in perfect continuity. The contributions of all writers who have helped to organize the scenario must be smoothly interwoven. The producer's assistants must blueprint and analyze every requirement in detail. Then they can forecast just how many days it should take to shoot the picture and what it will cost the studio for each day's shooting. The competent producer moves like a general, from objective to objective, with the aid of his staff of technical and creative workers.

After the shooting of the picture gets under way, the producer must continue to coordinate the contributions of many minds. He must see that the director works smoothly with his players and technicians. On viewing the results of each day's shooting in the next morning's "rushes," he must judge which shots secure the right effect for each scene. For the director takes numerous shots, of which only one will be used in the finished picture. The executive must be able to choose quickly the best "take" of each shot. One of the best tests of production skill, indeed, is a measure of the producer's ability to choose the right "takes" as the shooting progresses.

No matter how the producer may try to anticipate each production problem, many unforeseen issues arise. Under the high tension of studio activity, powerful personalities may clash and delay progress. The producer must be constantly alert and resourceful to keep things moving. When difficulties arise, he must meet them calmly and quickly. He is constantly concerned with completing the production within the limits of time and expense allotted to the picture.

If expensive scenes of mass action involving hundreds, perhaps thousands, of extra players are not completed on schedule, the producer may run into financial grief. Suppose a thousand extra players are enacting a battle scene which must be finished before sundown, and there remains less than an hour's work requiring bright sunlight. But the sun is rapidly sinking, and it may be necessary to pay the army of extras to return for another full day's work, just for a few final shots. Production costs may take an unexpected jump.

The ideal producer must therefore combine the skills of a general, a politician, a diplomat, a statesman, a businessman, and a showman.

Who are the best producers and which studios make the best pictures? Newspaper critics publish annual surveys. In New York the movie critics meet each year and vote. The National Board of Review expresses its opinions from year to year. The many thousands of workers who devote their lives to picture-making give their answers to these questions when the Academy of Motion Picture Arts and Sciences presents its annual array of "Oscars." The Academy awards are based on a secret ballot of the technical, artistic, and supervisory personnel of all the Hollywood studios. These people are the most expert judges of movies and of all the elements that go into movie production. Their opinions are independent, critical, and sincere. In 1948 they voted that the best picture was not a Hollywood production at all, but a film made in England, Laurence Olivier's *Hamlet*.

Since the inception of the awards in 1928, Metro-Goldwyn-Mayer pictures have been voted the best of the year six times, 20th Century-Fox pictures five times, Paramount and Columbia Pictures three times each, and Warner Brothers and Selznick productions twice each. RKO, Goldwyn, Universal, J. Arthur Rank, and Hecht-Lancaster have won the award once each.

By Academy standards, Metro makes the best pictures, and indeed that studio is generally regarded as having the most magnificent producing organization in the world. The distribution of awards to the other studios is a fair indication of the comparative excellence of films to be expected from these competing organizations.

Suggested Activities

1. Have you seen any film recently that has been remade on the basis of an older version? If so, what qualities does the story have that would have led the producer to suppose that he still owned a valuable property? List some films that you have seen during the past three years, the stories of which you believe will continue to be valuable movie properties in the years to come.

2. How much does a studio often invest in a major film? Look up the reported production costs of several of the recent and more spectacular motion pictures.

3. What effect do you think the competition of television now has upon production costs of motion pictures? Discuss the economics behind the reluctance of major studios to release their newer films for use in television.

5

Standards of Story Material

THE PRODUCTION of a photoplay begins with a *story idea*. The producer, in order to select a suitable story for his photoplay, reads synopses of many literary productions. The major studios in Hollywood maintain staffs of readers who make detailed synopses and analyses of many thousands of novels, plays, short stories, biographies, and non-fiction books.

Metro-Goldwyn-Mayer, for example, maintains a staff of sixty readers. These men and women are story analysts. Some of them specialize in telling stories orally. They present the highlights of stories under consideration at meetings of production executives. The selection of story material sometimes depends on the players whom the studio may have under contract and for whom the story may be suited.

In general, a producer looks for a story whose theme and treatment are fresh, timely, and of universal appeal. If the story is one for which the public has expressed its approval in unmistakable terms, the movie producer is interested in filming it. A play that has had a long run on Broadway or a book that has become a best-seller naturally interests movie executives.

However, even though a subject may be timely and pop-

Standards of Story Material • 35

ular, it may not be good screen material. It must be possible to *visualize* a story on the screen if it is to be useful as movie entertainment.

Furthermore, the story must be *free of the many taboos* which restrict the screen. The Production Code followed by Hollywood studios does not permit the screening of stories which may *offend* any nationality, race, or religion, or even any profession or occupation. The Legion of Decency of the Roman Catholic Church also maintains a careful watch over all movies and rates them from the standpoint of the church. Many movies have been rated as objectionable in part and some have been entirely condemned by church authorities. In addition, some of our states, including several large ones, have censorship boards. In 1952, however, in an epoch-making decision, the United States Supreme Court decided that no censor board could ban a movie on grounds that it was sacrilegious. This was based on the case of *The Miracle,* a film imported from Italy. Regardless of the court's decision, nevertheless, movie studios do their best to please, not to offend, the great masses of movie-goers throughout the world.

Producers must also make sure that any stories they buy are *free from plagiarism*. Lawsuits result from attempts to use story material to which studios may have no clear and exclusive right.

A story, to be screenable, must also be *free of libelous material*. Look up the meanings of these words in an unabridged dictionary: *taboo, plagiarism, libel*.

A screenplay is usually helped along by *good dialog*. If the lines which the characters speak in a play or a novel are lively, simple, clear to all, the story material is more appealing. But dialog, in a movie, can never be basic. It can only supplement or duplicate visual appeal.

After selecting a story to be screened, the producer assigns a scenario writer to the job of preparing a "shooting script." This is sometimes called a continuity. It tells, in *highly pictorial language,* exactly what we are to see on the screen. The script must be terse, smooth, and straightforward. Although some screenplays make use of the "flashback," most audiences prefer a narrative in strictly chronological order.

Additional writers, supplementing the work of the first scenarist, may contribute to the development of urgently needed visual action in the screenplay, so that the final result represents a synthesis of minds. The producer must harmonize the contributions of many individuals if he is to turn out a successful screening of the story. He recognizes that good scripts are not written, but rewritten. The best writers polish their own writing, indefatigably.

Some producers are also writers and directors, so that they dominate every detail of the production from start to finish. Many of the ablest writers in the picture business have become producer-directors. Their screen stories are usually constructed very logically.

The most popular types of stories have been those dealing with outdoor action, particularly stories of spectacular and romantic adventure. Other popular types are love stories, mystery melodramas, and comedies. Less popular, but appealing increasingly to intelligent audiences, are stories of social significance, sophisticated satires, and fantasies. For children, the most popular type of photoplay has long been the slapstick comedy, either in live-action or animated-cartoon form. Children love to have their slapstick presented in color, with lively music and sound effects. Photoplays based on famous fairy tales are of wide appeal to youngsters, if the films are made with imagination, lively action, and spectacular effects.

To be great, a photoplay must have *a great theme.* By

theme we mean the central idea of a story. The theme must be presented to us in a way that will startle us out of the ordinariness that besets our lives. A good photoplay excites us, inspires us.

It is unfortunately not easy to find screenable stories with great themes. Producers and writers for the popular screen do not as yet have the freedom of poets, novelists, playwrights, or even newspapermen. But as television tends to draw away from theaters the great audience of children and immature youth for whom many movies in the past have been made, there is likely to be an increase in the ratio of photoplays for people with more mature minds.

Let us hope that some movie-maker of the future may be able to follow the example of the great English poet, John Milton. When Milton was considering the selection of a subject for a great story, he felt at first that the story of King Arthur would make the greatest epic. He finally chose the story of the creation and fall of man. He wrote *Paradise Lost* because he felt that the theme of man's disobedience of God's commands presented the greatest challenge to a writer. He told the story of how Adam and Eve brought death into the world, "and all our woe." It remains for some future Milton of the screen to find a theme of similar greatness to be presented to the audiences of the world.

In judging story elements which you find in the movies, consider the significance of the main ideas around which the movies are built. Do they deal with cut-and-dried formulas, such as catching the criminal or winning the girl—adventures or romances that touch only the surface of life?

A poor story, even if given to a good director, will make a poor picture. The fundamental element of success in a photoplay is the quality of the story on the screen. The truly great movies are all basically good stories.

Suggested Activities

1. List some of your favorite books, stories, poems, or plays. In your opinion, which would make good movies? Why?

2. Make a list of criteria for a story that would be suitable for (a) your favorite movie actor and (b) your favorite movie actress. What personal characteristics do these stars have that would cause some stories to be unsuitable for them?

3. What is your favorite type of photoplay? Do other members of your family or your friends have different preferences? Discuss why a film may appeal to some people but not to others. Explain the lasting popularity of western movies.

6

Notable Screen Writers

WE HAVE SEEN that stories for the screen come from many sources. Great novels, short stories, and plays of the past, literary successes of our own day, or lively reports of current events may provide source material for movies. Many original stories are also written directly for the movies. Whatever the source, each story has to be translated into visual action. This means that the script must be developed in terms of the camera. Studios need imaginative screen playwrights who know what the camera can do and how to tell a story as a series of pictures.

Many of the best scenarists are old-timers in the field, having worked around studios in various capacities, learning the business from many angles. The services of the most successful of these writers are in such demand that they are under contract to devote almost their entire time to writing screenplays. They work in the specialized medium of motion pictures, rather than writing plays, novels, or short stories. Indeed, some screen writers specialize in one type of story, such as the outdoor action story.

Sometimes several writers work together. One, perhaps, works out the plot pictorially. Another develops bits of action or "business" to reveal characterizations. A third may polish up bits of comedy dialog. The writer or writers must work closely with the producer or the director or both. The final result is a *shooting script* that provides detailed and specific directions for making each scene, including settings, camera angles, facial expressions or dramatic action, dialog, time of day or night, and sound effects, so that players, cameramen, sound engineers, and all others concerned may understand exactly the effects desired.

In the days of D. W. Griffith, the director frequently made up his dialog and invented new situations as he went along. Today no director would begin work without a highly detailed script to follow, even though he may depart from it or add new scenes as the shooting develops. The director must be thoroughly acquainted with the script and satisfied with it. The need for close coordination of effort in film-making has resulted in director-and-writer teams.

One such successful team, not so long ago, was composed of John Ford and Dudley Nichols. Nichols wrote scripts for many of the best Ford films, including *The Lost Patrol, The Informer, Stagecoach, The Long Voyage Home,* and *The Fugitive.* That does not mean, of course, that Nichols originated the stories. He took the stories and adapted them for the screen.

Nichols became a producer-director, as many of the best writers often do. He was responsible for writing, directing, and producing *Sister Kenny* and *Mourning Becomes Electra.* His career as a writer prepared him to assume the job of carrying his film story to completion.

Another such team was formed by Frank Capra and Robert Riskin. Riskin worked as a writer with Director Capra on *It Happened One Night, Mr. Deeds Goes to Town, You Can't Take It With You, Lost Horizon,* and *Meet John Doe.* How much of the wit and pathos that characterize most of these successful pictures is due to the director and how much to the writer would be hard to say. With such a team, the final result is truly a cooperative effort.

Charles Brackett and Billy Wilder formed a writing team in which one member produced while the other directed their joint scripts. As collaborators, they wrote scripts for many successful movies. The Academy Award for the best picture of 1945 went to their screen version of Charles Jackson's novel, *The Lost Weekend*, written by the pair and directed by Wilder. Brackett served as producer for their large-scale Bing Crosby musical, *Emperor Waltz*. They also collaborated to write, produce, and direct *Miss Tatlock's Millions* and *A Foreign Affair*.

Two other excellent writers who have become directors and producers are Nunnally Johnson and Preston Sturges. Johnson's scripts for such outstanding pictures as *The Grapes of Wrath, The Moon Is Down, Along Came Jones* and *The Dark Mirror* earned him high regard in Hollywood. He served as producer as well as writer of *The Woman in the Window, Mr. Peabody and the Mermaid,* and *Three Came Home*. Sturges has specialized in a kind of comedy that is full of broad satire. Among pictures written and directed by him are *The Miracle of Morgan's Creek* and *The Beautiful Blonde from Bashful Bend*.

Attempts have been made to secure scenarists by bringing out to Hollywood writers who have made successes in the field of the novel, the short story, or the stage-play. Many such writers have served only short terms in the studios and then returned to their regular work, finding that their talents were not suited to writing directly for the screen. Others have remained to share their work among film producers, publishers, and stage-play producers. A few have become entirely devoted to the writing of screenplays.

Ben Hecht is one of the most successful screen writers among those who served apprenticeships elsewhere. When he began to give all his time to the screen, he became famous for such pictures as *Notorious,* and, as co-writer, *Ride the Pink Horse.* As producer and director as well as writer, he was responsible for *Specter of the Rose,* a picture which was a critical success but too adult in its appeal to be a popular success.

Some well-known writers who have divided their work between the screen and other media are Sally Benson, who collaborated on *Shadow of a Doubt* and *Anna and the King of Siam;* Stephen Longstreet, who wrote *The Jolson Story;* R. C. Sherriff, who wrote *Odd Man Out* and *Quartet;* and Robert E. Sherwood, who wrote *The Best Years of Our Lives.*

The writer plays a major role in turning out a first-rate film. Students who are trying to develop a better understanding of what contributes to a good motion picture should pay increasing attention to the sources of screen stories and should note among the screen credits the persons responsible for adapting them to screen use.

Suggested Activities

1. Why do some successful writers of stage-plays, short stories, and novels fail in their attempts to write successful screenplays? List some of the ways in which screen writing differs from other kinds of story-telling.

2. Compare a recent picture with the story or play on which it was based. What does each have that the other doesn't? What did the scenarist add, omit, or change? Can you suggest reasons for the changes? Were the changes justifiable?

3. Compile a list of books that have recently served as literary sources of motion pictures. Post this list on your classroom bulletin board or in your school library as a suggested reading list.

4. Locate an example of a recent motion-picture scenario. Study it for the differences between a screenplay and a stageplay. Report to the class on the differences you find.

7

Standards of Direction

THE MOST SIGNIFICANT quality in a movie director is *imagination*. If the story excites his imagination and he is genuinely interested in the theme of the film, he is likely to have something sincere to express on the screen. If he lacks the all-important creative imagination necessary to impart excitement to the filming of the script, or if he does not sincerely believe in the story, he will be unable to make audiences laugh or cry or feel thrilled or impressed with what they see on the screen.

His job is to bring the scenario to life, to visualize what is called for in the script. He must interpret the story uniquely in terms of the screen. He must appeal primarily to the eye, so that even a deaf person can understand the key scenes. But even if the director has a strong visual sense, he will fail if he does not choose just the right camera angles. He must help audiences to identify themselves with the characters, to feel the emotions which the characters experience, to see the action through the eyes of the players. In this way he builds sympathetic interest in the characters.

To present a true picture of life as portrayed in the story, a director must be acquainted with that kind of life. To this end he may have to do much reading and research among original sources. He may also have to spend some months on location studying people of the type represented in the story, absorbing atmosphere and gaining an intimate knowledge of his subject.

A good director can make the screen story flow along with the continuity of a river. He can give the action a kind of rhythm or movement, such as we find in a ballet or a musical composition. In some photoplays, notably in animated cartoons and musical productions, the director may begin with music and fit the action to the musical themes and ideas. The more closely the director approaches a *continuous flow of rhythmic action,* the closer he comes to expressing his ideas in terms of the poetry of pure cinema. For this reason many directors like to include scenes of dancing in their films. Many of the scenes in the comedies of Charles Chaplin and of René Clair move with the rhythm of a dance. The motion pictures of Robert Flaherty are filmic poems.

One often hears the expression "directorial touches." Have you ever been surprised by striking bits of action which tell much in brief footage on the screen? A newspaper blown along the gutter, revealing a headline at a critical moment in the story; a glove or handkerchief significantly left behind; the reaction of a dog to a dramatic situation; the doll left behind by an injured child; the rhythmic squeak of a rocking chair—these touches at critical moments in the story bring tears or laughter from audiences. They delight us, startle us, with the clever way in which the director uses them to reveal plot points or to develop characterization. These brief scenes, if presented with a light touch and without recourse to exaggerated action or physical violence, are *very valuable in screen technique.* However, such touches alone cannot make a picture good. The director's chief aim must be to tell a coherent and well-balanced story. The movie as a whole must satisfy the audience. The whole is necessarily greater than any of its parts, no matter how good those parts may be.

To this end the director rehearses scene after scene until it is played smoothly, naturally, and convincingly—always bearing in mind what he must emphasize in relation to the complete photoplay. Every bit of action or dialog must be well-timed and must contribute to the desired effect before it is recorded.

To win inspired performances from his players, the director must himself feel inspired with the subject he is filming. He must command the respect of powerful personalities who enact the parts. His must be the master mind. He must control the players so that they will work in harmony with one another during the filming and produce the all-important effect.

Like the coach of a crack athletic team, he must watch his players and protect them from one another and even from themselves. He must keep them from risking costly injuries by seeing that they are always within the bounds of safety. He must exercise restraint over scenes of fast or violent action, using camera tricks to secure effects of speed while the players actually move slowly and precisely. He must be patient and sympathetic, yet persistent, at times guiding his players like a teacher who develops to the utmost the talents of superior students, whose gifts may excel the teacher's.

Directors often find it easier to handle talented children and old character actors than stars who are at the height of their power. Players must be handled with tact, but they must inevitably follow the director's thinking if he is to secure the effects he is after.

Likewise, the director must collaborate with technicians on the set, particularly his head cameraman, who must work out just the right lighting effects. The director knows what lighting and what viewpoints are appropriate to the mood, atmosphere, and dramatic emphasis of each scene. He must show the cameraman what are *the most telling angles* for shooting a given scene. The good director can present important stars so that they look their best. Likewise, make-up artists, costume designers, sound-recording engineers, decorators, and scenic architects all contribute to the effect which the masterful director is seeking.

Often a director can devise realistic sound effects to help tell the story. Background musical effects, unnoticed by the audience and usually added after the film has been edited, help to give emotional quality to a scene and to enhance the effect of dialog. Sometimes a blind man will understand from the sound alone what is going on in a good movie.

From the standpoint of pleasing the financial authorities, represented by the producer, the big problem of the director is *to adhere to the time-schedule* for shooting his picture. He must try to finish the film within a specified number of days. While aiming to proceed with due speed and economy in securing his effects, however, the director cannot afford to sacrifice effectiveness for the sake of speed. Thus he is sometimes "between the devil and the deep sea" when he encounters delays. But if he is wise, he will never let anything interfere with his aim to make a successful picture, regardless of the urgency for speed. Some studios, like M-G-M, are famous for allowing directors extra time when it becomes clear that by remaking some scenes a fair picture can be converted into a really good one. This is a smart policy in film-making. A director who is hurried or too easily satisfied may lose the money invested in an expensive production. The director must work for economy of effect, yet avoid false economy.

From day to day he views the "rushes" so that he may know how well he is achieving the effects he desires. He tries to make each scene as effective as possible, and yet avoid *shots that may be censorable.* Objectionable scenes, in the end, may only land on the cutting-room floor. Such cutting may weaken or destroy the coherence of the story and may require expensive re-shooting.

A director must be sufficiently cost-conscious also to avoid striving for so-called "arty" effects *which do not advance the story.* He is more successful if he considers himself a craftsman who follows principles of showmanship. *His aim must be to please audiences rather than his own artistic instincts.* Whereas an artist essentially pleases himself, the maker of a popular photoplay must find his pleasure in pleasing the public. If a director is to bring his studio a profit on an investment of a million dollars or more, he must bow to the sovereignty of the box-office.

One way of economizing in movie-making, aside from avoiding shots which are not essential to the story, is to use shrewd judgment in the sequence of shots. A director who is sure of his aims can do considerable editing as he goes along. On the other hand, a worried and uncertain director may waste time by shooting from angles which later cannot be used. The expense of numerous "protection shots" can be forgiven only in a big picture made by an ace director who is always working for mass appeal.

When a director has become outstandingly successful, he may become the producer of his own pictures. He may set up an independent organization, or a unit in the studio where he has been working. Such a director then becomes solely responsible for the quality of the work he turns out. However, a great director, even when he works under the supervision of a producer, may have much to say as to the budget and may dominate every detail. Such directors may develop brilliant teams of writers and stars with whom they work. Out of such teams have come some of the finest pictures.

Every good director has his own style and his own methods. Some directors like to control each gesture, each movement, each intonation of an actor's voice. Others like to give competent players freedom to do creative work in the hope that this will result in more sincere performances. Some directors give cameramen and cutters scope. Others supervise closely every detail of photography and editing.

The style of a director and the relative emphasis he gives to various elements of a picture are often rooted in his background. If he was previously an ace cameraman, like Victor Fleming, who directed *Gone With the Wind,* he tends to emphasize cinematography. If he was previously a writer, like Joseph L. Mankiewicz, he tends to emphasize logical story-construction and bright dialog. If he was previously an actor, like Frank Lloyd, who directed *Mutiny on the Bounty,* he tends to rehearse and polish each gesture and each line of dialog until he is completely satisfied with the performance. If he was previously an editor or cutter, like Lewis Milestone, who directed *All Quiet on the Western Front,* he will emphasize smooth continuity. If he has been an artist or has been brought up among artists like Jean Renoir, who directed *The River,* he will emphasize artistic pictorial effects of composition, rhythmic action, striking use of color and portrait-like close-ups. If he was a supervisor of staging and dancing, like Vincente Minnelli, who directed *An American in Paris,* he will excel in spectacular effects, especially dance numbers.

By becoming acquainted with the biographies and achievements of important directors, we shall be better able to appreciate their work in each new film that we see.

Suggested Activities

1. How do the responsibilities of directors differ in the fields of the motion-picture, television, radio, and stage production? Compare these fields in terms of such factors as (a) time involved in preparing the final product for the public, (b) amount of money invested, and (c) number of persons under the supervision of the director.

2. If you were preparing to become a director of motion pictures, what kinds of experience do you think would be of greatest value to you? Explain what you think each experience would contribute to the skills needed by a good director.

3. Make a list of recent award-winning movie directors. Then prepare a report on the biography of one of them, using such reference books as *Current Biography* and *Who's Who in America*. Write to the director, asking him what is one of his favorite pictures and what elements he particularly likes in that picture. Include his response in your report.

4. Find examples among recent pictures to illustrate the point that a director's background influences his style.

Notable Photoplay Directors

LET US CONSIDER the work of five film directors who achieved early success before sound came in and who have continued as important men: Cecil DeMille, King Vidor, Michael Curtiz, Fritz Lang, and Lewis Milestone. DeMille, by 1930, had established a reputation for turning out spectacular pictures with historical or religious backgrounds. Major productions of his during the past two decades have included *The Sign of the Cross* (1932), *Cleopatra* (1934), *The Crusades* (1935), *The Plainsman* (1936), *Union Pacific* (1939), *Reap the Wild Wind* (1942), *Unconquered* (1947), *Samson and Delilah* (1949), *The Greatest Show on Earth* (1952), and *The Ten Commandments* (1956).

DeMille's pictures specialize in spectacular settings on colossal stages, with scenes requiring thousands of players. He emphasizes colorful costumes. He depicts tremendous catastrophes or epic achievements.

For years before a DeMille picture reaches the screen, it is heralded through the press. Statistics on the number of actors required and the amount of money spent on preparation for making the film become familiar to the readers of movie columns in newspapers and publicity articles in fan magazines.

52 • Standards of Photoplay Appreciation

The studio spares no expense in making the picture truly spectacular. DeMille is a masterful director of big scenes. It was he who first used a megaphone to give directions. He was the first to install a public-address system on a movie lot to control mass action. DeMille's name on a picture is more prominent than that of any of his stars. This is rarely true of other directors. DeMille dominates the entire film, feeling sure that he knows what the great public wants. He is the "master showman." The public has come to know what to expect from his pictures.

Few of DeMille's pictures had much good said about them by serious critics until 1952, when he won the Academy Award. Sometimes the critics have praised the splendor of his films as far as settings and costumes are concerned. Generally critics have spoken of DeMille pictures as belonging more to the classification of spectacles, to be admired and gaped at, but scarcely to be remembered as significant. However, the DeMille pictures have been highly successful. They capitalize upon some of the basic values of the motion picture, its appeal of pageantry, color, and exotic sights. DeMille is truly a great showman.

King Vidor, who has been less active in recent years than DeMille, has won a far different reputation. He has been known for the realism of his story-telling. One of his early successes, *The Big Parade* (1925), dealt with the life of the soldier in World War I; and while it would be regarded today as rather sentimental, for its time it was thought unusually frank. A picture that is sometimes regarded as Vidor's most creative film, *The Crowd* (1928), happened to come at a time when the fact that it was silent kept it from much notice except among critics. In this film, Vidor attempted to show an ordinary man's fear of being lost in the great masses of humanity that crowd the cities. He used some of the symbolic techniques that were notable in *The Cabinet of Dr. Caligari.*

Other notable films directed by King Vidor include *Hallelujah* (1930), in which there was an all-Negro cast; *Street Scene* (1931), an adaptation of an Elmer Rice play; *The Citadel* (1938); *H. M. Pulham, Esq.* (1941); and *The Fountainhead* (1949). Vidor will be remembered as one of the first important directors to believe that the screen could be used to tell a socially significant story; that is, have something serious to say about the problems of mankind. His greatest achievement is the screen version of Tolstoy's *War and Peace* (1956).

Another old-timer is Fritz Lang, who was one of the outstanding German directors whose work of the early twenties was so influential. Lang's early German pictures included *Siegfried, Metropolis,* and *M,* all of which remain of great interest to the serious student of film art. When Lang was brought to this country in the thirties, he was already known as a "director's director." The dramatic quality of his work, the fast pace, the emphasis on mood, have been much admired. Among his best-known pictures made in the United States are *Fury* (1936), which dealt with a lynching; *You Only Live Once* (1937); *Man Hunt* (1941); *The Ministry of Fear* (1945); *Cloak and Dagger* (1946); and *The Secret Beyond the Door* (1948).

Michael Curtiz, another import from Europe, has been one of the busiest directors in Hollywood, having made nearly eighty films since 1931. Known for his spectacular scenes, his DeMille-ish talents in the Hungarian and French movies he made before coming to this country, he has since developed a breadth of style that makes it possible for him to work on a great variety of stories. He is known as a perfectionist, demanding from his actors the very best they can do. However, little footage is wasted in a Curtiz film: when the camera starts to work, the scene it takes is likely to be just the proper length. Curtiz is noted for "camera-cutting," that is, taking only the film that will actually be needed. This ability comes from his vast skill and experience. He is proud of the economy with which he can secure a desired effect. Like other important directors, Curtiz is his own producer, even within the framework of the Warner Brothers studio.

Notable Curtiz films include *Private Lives of Elizabeth and Essex* (1939), *Black Fury* (1935), *Casablanca* (1943), *Mildred Pierce* (1945), *Life with Father* (1947), and *Young Man with a Horn* (1950). His directing of *Casablanca* won a Motion Picture Academy Award.

Lewis Milestone is the fifth of the earlier group of directors. Known as a careful and competent worker, Milestone's value was widely recognized by the time he shared with another director the first award made by the Motion Picture Academy in 1928. His famous picture, *All Quiet on the Western Front,* won him his second directing award in 1930. It revealed his remarkable psychological skill in portraying the intimate qualities of men in war regardless of which side they were on. The real villain, he showed, was war itself. We may consider him typical of the many fine directors who have turned out good pictures during the last quarter-century.

A second group of directors may be thought of as those who have followed upon the footsteps of the older and more experienced ones. The four chosen to represent this group have shared among them more directing awards from the Motion Picture Academy than any others that could be named. John Ford has won the award four times; Frank Capra, three times; Leo McCarey and William Wyler, twice.

John Ford won the Academy Award for directing *The Informer* (1935), *Grapes of Wrath* (1940), *How Green Was My Valley* (1941), and *The Quiet Man* (1953). *The In-*

former, made from a novel by Liam O'Flaherty, was characterized by the magnificent acting of Victor McLaglen as traitor to the Irish cause, and by lighting and pace that have kept the picture on the screen as a classic. *Grapes of Wrath* was notable for its realism and the success with which the social message of John Steinbeck's story was translated into a new medium. *How Green Was My Valley* was another instance in which Ford made a significant novel equally meaningful on the screen.

In all of Ford's films, there is dramatic and memorable photography. Two of his less popular films, *The Long Voyage Home* (1940) and *The Fugitive* (1947), are among the most beautiful motion pictures ever made. Ford's effects do not depend upon tricky angle shots or a roving camera. Frequently in the long shots of which he is fond in his outdoor pictures, the camera remains in one place, with a magnificently framed composition, while the action occurs within the frame. Ford, who now works through his own company, demands as much of his cameramen and experts in lighting as did D. W. Griffith.

One of the types which Ford has been responsible for bringing to new heights is that old favorite, the western. Beginning with *Stagecoach* (1939), which still is a money-maker, he has turned out a number of westerns which have given new dignity to one of the most popular types of entertainment. To make it possible to film artistic successes like *The Fugitive,* the industry has capitalized upon his flair for action stories with *My Darling Clementine* (1946), *Fort Apache* (1948), and *She Wore a Yellow Ribbon* (1949). In these films, the scope and beauty of the outdoors are made so much a part of the story that they are worth seeing for their backgrounds alone.

Ford built up around him a team of actors, sometimes

called Ford's Stock Company. Among them were McLaglen, John Wayne, Henry Fonda, and Ward Bond, along with a number of other character actors. In addition, Ford collaborated closely with a top-notch script-writer, Dudley Nichols. Together, this team turned out some of the most rewarding films. Ford keenly realizes what are the essential values of the motion picture. He likes scope and action; he sees the camera as a reporter of truth and beauty; he minimizes dialog and lets what happens tell the story for him.

Quite a different approach has been that of Frank Capra, whose Academy prize-winners are *It Happened One Night* (1934), *Mr. Deeds Goes to Town* (1936), and *You Can't Take It With You* (1938). Sometimes referred to as the "O. Henry of the Screen," Capra is at his best as a humorist. He has the knack of giving his stories a fresh twist that marks the born teller of humorous stories. His writer, Robert Riskin, worked very closely on many of the Capra successes.

Capra got his start in movies as a "gag" man for Mack Sennett. His job was to think up funny situations for the old two-reel comedies. From there he advanced to director of comedy shorts, from which he was graduated to feature director. In addition to being distinguished for the wittiness of his stories, Capra has combined a kind of social satire that first appeared in an early success, *Lady for a Day* (1933). In several films he tried to point toward the need for good people to become more interested in contributing to the common welfare. These are *Mr. Smith Goes to Washington* (1939), *Meet John Doe* (1941), *It's a Wonderful Life* (1946), and *State of the Union* (1948).

Capra combines humor and warmth in a way that makes his carefully planned pictures great popular successes.

Another successful director is William Wyler, whose prize-winning pictures are *Mrs. Miniver* (1942) and *The Best*

Years of Our Lives (1946). Both of these films were produced by Samuel Goldwyn, as were other Wyler successes, such as *Dodsworth* (1936), *Dead End* (1937), *Wuthering Heights* (1939), and *The Little Foxes* (1941). Assured the best of care in story selection and screen adaptation as well as in choice of cast, Wyler turned out one artistic and popular success after another, under the Goldwyn aegis.

Leo McCarey is another maker of popular hits. His prize-winning pictures include *The Awful Truth* (1937) and *Going My Way* (1944). Each of these pictures introduced a new type of comedy. *The Awful Truth,* with Irene Dunne and Cary Grant, was the first of a cycle of hilarious comedies built around ridiculous situations and depending for their humor on sparkling dialog and clever characterization. *Going My Way* combined humor and pathos in a religious background that was followed not only by McCarey's own *The Bells of St. Mary's* (1945) but by a number of similar pictures by different directors. McCarey probably ranks next to Capra in combining wit and warmth in pictures that go straight to the hearts of audiences.

Perhaps belonging in this group of highly successful directors is Alfred Hitchcock. The reason Hitchcock has been passed by for Academy Awards is that his specialty does not lend itself to serious consideration. He is the greatest of all directors of mystery stories, but he seems often interested in suspense for its own sake. Beginning with his first notable success, *The Thirty-Nine Steps* (1935), made while he was in England, he has turned out many thrillers and chillers of exceptional quality. Some of these are *Rebecca* (1940), *Suspicion* (1941), *Saboteur* (1942), *Spellbound* (1945), *The Paradine Case* (1948), *The Rope* (1949). *The Rear Window* (1954) and *To Catch a Thief* (1955) have added to Hitchcock's reputation.

Hitchcock films are full of surprises, many of them depending upon skillful use of camera shots to shock the spectator. Hitchcock has taken the principle of suspense as developed early by Griffith and made of it the backbone for his stories. By careful preparation, he succeeds in making us wonder whether all will come out right, until the suspense becomes almost unbearable. The skill in this field that once was largely Hitchcock's has now been studied by many others. The thriller in the Hitchcock tradition is the stock-in-trade of several other directors today.

Finally we may deal more briefly with a few newer directors who have attracted a good deal of critical attention: John Huston, Elia Kazan, Sir Carol Reed, and Michael Powell.

John Huston won Academy Awards with *The Treasure of Sierra Madre* in 1948, both for having directed it and for having written the script. This picture, starring Humphrey Bogart and the director's father, Walter Huston, was noteworthy for its swift pace and realism. An earlier picture, *The Maltese Falcon* (1941), was one of the first of the hard-boiled killer-dillers that have since become a staple product of the movie-houses. Huston is one of the most talented directors in the world. His recent pictures include *The Red Badge of Courage* (1951), *The African Queen* (1952), *Moulin Rouge* (1953), and *Moby Dick* (1956).

Elia Kazan, whose *Gentleman's Agreement* (1947) and *On the Waterfront* (1954) won him Oscars, is a successful director of stage plays in New York as well as of motion pictures. At present he is dividing his time between the two occupations. His pictures include also *A Tree Grows in Brooklyn* (1945), *Boomerang* (1947), *Pinky* (1949), and *East of Eden* (1955).

Sir Carol Reed is an English director whose best-known films are fairly recent: *Odd Man Out* (1947), *The Fallen*

Idol (1949), *The Third Man* (1950), and *Trapeze* (1956). He has probably received more critical acclaim than any other younger director. *The Fallen Idol,* with its remarkably sustained picture of a domestic tragedy seen through the eyes of a child, was marked by expert acting performances and highly intelligent writing. *The Third Man,* a more widely popular picture, was remarkable for the extraordinary photography of Robert Krasker, in which scene after scene was rendered memorable, and for the haunting theme music played on the zither. Reed is already so well known that his name joins the select list of those directors who are featured in the advertising in type-sizes larger than those of their stars.

A less well-known English director, Michael Powell, concludes our list of younger directors. His best-known films are *Stairway to Heaven* (1946), *Black Narcissus* (1947), and *Red Shoes* (1948). Not all of these have been widely distributed in the United States. However, Powell's name is one to watch for. His pictures are characterized by effective writing, done by Emeric Pressburger, whose name is featured with the director's, and by a certain delicacy or charm that contrasts greatly with the more violent emphasis, at times, on blood-and-thunder in American pictures.

In addition to the directors to whom we have given some attention, there are many others of importance like Joseph L. Mankiewicz and George Stevens, whose appeal is growing yearly. Each year the *Film Daily Year Book* lists the credits of about 300 directors. The Hollywood directors maintain an excellent professional organization, The Screen Directors' Guild, Inc., which is glad to send information on directors to students of the motion picture. Directors whose productions are leading box-office successes are listed by *Motion Picture Herald* as "champions" from month to month. At the end of the year the trade annual *Fame* lists the "champions of champions" from the trade point of view. However, the criterion of the box-office is not the criterion of the classroom. It is an indication of commercial success only, revealing the trend of public taste.

Since the inception of the Academy Awards in 1928, annual Oscars have been awarded to directors as follows:

1928 Frank Borzage, *Seventh Heaven,* and Lewis Milestone, *Two Arabian Knights.*
1929 Frank Lloyd, *Divine Lady.*
1930 Lewis Milestone, *All Quiet on the Western Front.*
1931 Norman Taurog, *Skippy.*
1932 Frank Borzage, *Bad Girl.*
1933 Frank Lloyd, *Cavalcade.*
1934 Frank Capra, *It Happened One Night.*
1935 John Ford, *The Informer.*
1936 Frank Capra, *Mr. Deeds Goes to Town.*
1937 Leo McCarey, *The Awful Truth.*
1938 Frank Capra, *You Can't Take It With You.*
1939 Victor Fleming, *Gone With the Wind.*
1940 John Ford, *The Grapes of Wrath.*
1941 John Ford, *How Green Was My Valley.*
1942 William Wyler, *Mrs. Miniver.*
1943 Michael Curtiz, *Casablanca.*
1944 Leo McCarey, *Going My Way.*
1945 Billy Wilder, *The Lost Weekend.*
1946 William Wyler, *The Best Years of Our Lives.*
1947 Elia Kazan, *Gentleman's Agreement.*
1948 John Huston, *The Treasure of Sierra Madre.*
1949 Joseph L. Mankiewicz, *A Letter to Three Wives.*
1950 Joseph L. Mankiewicz, *All About Eve.*
1951 George Stevens, *A Place in the Sun.*
1952 John Ford, *The Quiet Man.*

1953 Fred Zinnemann, *From Here to Eternity*.
1954 Elia Kazan, *On the Waterfront*.
1955 Delbert Mann, *Marty*.

By Academy standards the best director is four-time winner John Ford. Other good directors are three-time winner Frank Capra; two-time winners Frank Borzage, Lewis Milestone, Frank Lloyd, Leo McCarey, William Wyler, Elia Kazan and Joseph L. Mankiewicz; and one-time winners Norman Taurog, Victor Fleming, Michael Curtiz, Billy Wilder, George Stevens, John Huston, Fred Zinnemann, and Delbert Mann.

Of the many persons concerned with ensuring that a motion picture shall have genuine value, the most intimately concerned is the director. Upon his skill, judgment, and good taste depends the quality of the final product. Therefore, discriminating movie-goers should become well acquainted with the names and achievements of the outstanding directors. Choosing a motion picture to see on the basis of who directed it is the surest way to make a wise selection.

Suggested Activities

1. Choose one of the directors discussed in this chapter and look up added information about his achievements. Report your findings to the class.
2. Study the advertising of current films in your local newspapers or in an issue of a magazine. How many of the films have directors whose names are featured in the advertising? What does that tell you about the probable reputation of the director? About public taste?
3. The next time you see a motion picture, notice where the name of the director of the film comes in the list of

"credits" with which the film opens. Why does his name occupy this position?

4. What do movie stars have to say about the directors with whom they have worked? See whether you can locate such remarks in the books available to you or in newspaper and magazine articles about new film productions.

5. How often are references made to directors in gossip columns from Hollywood? Collect a number of such columns and mark the references you find. Post these columns on the classroom bulletin board with your comments.

6. Interview a number of other students or five or six adults in your neighborhood as to their knowledge of outstanding motion-picture directors. Several members of the class may combine forces to carry out a series of such interviews. What conclusions do you come to from a study of the responses you have gathered?

9

Standards of Photoplay Acting

The most important quality in an actor is strength of personality. Since the essence of drama is conflict, an actor must be aggressive when necessary. Unless he enjoys dramatic clash, he cannot do justice to scenes of strong emotion. Even though he may portray the character of a weakling, the player himself can be no weakling.

Most actors have winning qualities of personal magnetism. They have an appealing charm which makes them likable. They enjoy the spirit of make-believe. They like to entertain people, to dominate and spellbind audiences.

Good actors must be able not only to portray dynamic characters; they must also be able to listen to others with intense concentration. Some of the finest acting is not acting at all, but reacting; that is, cooperating in dialog by appearing as an unusually good listener.

Great actors are acutely observant of the mannerisms of many kinds of people. They like to watch people and to imitate them. They can select the most significant details which characterize personality, so as to emphasize these in holding up the mirror to life.

A motion-picture actor, besides having these general qualities, must be photogenic. This means he must photograph well from many angles. The camera must find his face expressive. His eyes particularly must be able to express subtle shades of meaning. In close-ups he must be able to reveal the very soul of a character by the expression in his eyes. The motion-picture camera is a searching instrument. Therefore, a player who is obviously artificial is not convincing on the screen.

If an actor is not really capable of feeling a wide range of emotions, he will lack emotional power. To understand the joys, fears, and sorrows of the human heart which he must portray, he must himself have had experience or observation of such emotions and sufficient understanding of them to give them convincing expression on the screen.

The best actors are people of quick sympathy. Their emotional power is genuine because they have insight into the hearts of people. They understand what makes people happy or sad. They can sympathize with children, animals, old people, rich people, poor people, unusual people.

A movie actor must also be able to take direction quickly and intelligently. Many directors insist on dominating every detail of an actor's performance. Every move, every camera angle, every step and gesture is usually worked out so completely in the director's mind that all the actor need do is to follow directions and concentrate on performance, giving all he has to the portrayal of emotion.

This is not to say that an actor may allow himself to be a mere puppet in the hands of a director. He must be able to evolve, out of the exacting routine imposed by the director, a convincing performance that will move audiences to tears or laughter. He must be a conscious artist, genuinely creative, giving expression to the director's conception of the part. This is not easy in a motion-picture studio, because the actor in a studio does not have the advantages of an actor on the stage. In a stage-play, the player has the benefit of mass audience reaction at each performance and can be guided by it.

In motion-picture acting, a player must have a particularly acute sense of rhythmic movement, of split-second timing of that movement, as well as perfection in speaking lines. Unless he has extraordinary talent for precise give-and-take, he will not be able to make just the right oral and visual responses at exactly the right time. Even though he may know the techniques of cinematic pantomime, even if his bodily movements are in themselves expressive, he will unfortunately create the wrong effect if his timing is imperfect.

In a motion-picture studio, the stage is usually cluttered with paraphernalia, but no matter how much the confusion, no matter how cramped the studio conditions, the actor must maintain complete self-control and poise. Although surrounded by confusing spotlights, reflectors, and cables, as well as the all-seeing eyes of cameras and the supersensitive ears of microphones, he must remain casual, natural, spontaneous. There must be no hint on the screen of the mechanization and the intense lighting of the movie-stage.

Acting is hard work. It requires long, hard rehearsals. An actor must therefore be physically able to meet such arduous requirements by maintaining health and vigor. If his vitality slips, he will not be able to transmute the hard discipline of his craft into something beautiful, exciting, and entertaining on the screen.

From the standpoint of the audience, a player must be fundamentally fit for the part. If he is handicapped by being miscast, his job will be vastly more difficult. He may be unable to overcome this handicap, and the effect will be unconvincing. Producers and directors are, of course, keenly aware that a player must be physically, mentally, and emotionally suited to a part. Producers test numerous possible players before selecting the best one to undertake the interpretation of even a minor role. In casting a player, a studio considers his face, build, height, weight, voice, age, and background. Even if a player seems physically suited to a part, his mental disposition and known personality may not meet the requirements. At times special talents are also needed for enacting a role, such as skills in fencing, riding, swimming, dancing, singing, or oratory. All good players are not equipped with these abilities, but some are apt and can be trained.

There is a tendency to "type" players in Hollywood, but many are quite versatile. George Sanders, for example, has an excellent singing voice, suitable even for grand opera; he has succeeded in portraying a great variety of dramatic roles on the screen, ranging from the extreme polish of drawing-room comedy to the rugged individualism of an artistic genius who goes off to paint in the solitude of a South Sea island. Other players of great versatility are Olivia de Havilland, Alec Guinness, Vivien Leigh, Fredric March, Charles Laughton, and, more recently, Bing Crosby. Can you mention others?

Of course an actor in the movies is greatly aided by experts in make-up and costume. Studios have advanced the art of make-up to the point where players may be made to look like well-known historical personages with no trace of artificiality. Knowing that his appearance will be convincing, an actor is completely at ease in assuming the role of an outstanding hero, such as Abraham Lincoln or Andrew Jackson. Likewise, the art of costuming, even in photoplays dealing with periods when costumes were very elaborate, has been perfected for the screen. Costumes can be simplified to allow actors to feel natural in them and yet create the effect of the historic period.

Nevertheless, a good player must be able to submerge his own personality in the particular part he is playing. He must be able, if necessary, to assume a foreign accent or a peculiar mannerism of speech and rehearse it until he seems "to the manner born." If the audience notices that the special mannerisms are merely assumed, the effect will be comic.

Some screen actors have such strong personalities that they are at their best when permitted to play themselves rather than compelled to submerge their personalities. If an actor's personality shines through make-up and costumes, if we are unable to forget the actor, we fail to get the required portrayal of the character. A true actor sheds his own personality as a snake sheds its skin. Such an actor gets inside the heart and soul of the character he is presenting. His performance is a deeply mental one, not merely physical, acrobatic, superficial. A conscientious player studies the character he enacts as deeply as possible, wants to know all about the background of that character, how he developed, what his life history has been. He likes to discuss the character from every possible angle, so that he may live the part. Such a player uses the Stanislavsky method of acting. This method takes much more time than the usual Hollywood methods permit, but it results in such realistic performances that the player can improvise action that will be true to the character.

A good actor does not perform as a soloist, but reacts to the other characters in the scene. He contributes always to the photoplay as a whole. He sees the implications of each situation through the eyes of the character he represents, but he is able to identify himself with other characters. He must do all he can to interpret the meaning and spirit of the story, to do his part toward making the theme of the photoplay luminous.

68 • Standards of Photoplay Appreciation

Suggested Activities

1. Look up more information about the Stanislavsky method of acting and report on this to the class. Consult books on dramatic art for this project.

2. What are some of the ways in which make-up can be used to alter an actor's appearance to fit the needs of a particular role? Gather information on this topic by use of the *Readers' Guide to Periodical Literature,* which lists recent articles by topics.

3. Choose a play, novel, or short-story known to all members of the class. How would you cast this story from among the movie stars you know? Compare your casting choices with those of other students in the class.

4. How do the requirements for acting differ between stage and screen? Discuss the reasons why some popular film stars fail on the stage and some popular stage stars fail in the movies. Name some actors and actresses who have been equally successful in both. Why have they succeeded in both fields?

5. From your library or from the Academy of Motion Picture Arts and Sciences in Hollywood obtain a list of players who have won awards for their performances. Report to the class on the qualities which made one or two of the performances of prize-winning caliber.

10

Notable Screen Actors

A SERIOUS STUDENT of motion pictures once wrote an article entitled, "Are Actors Necessary?" He was thinking of the fact that in the movies a mule can talk, a squirrel can dance, and Mickey Mouse can cover the range of known emotions. Animals and babies, unconscious of the camera, often make very natural actors. The collie in *Lassie;* the bulls in *Pandora, Quo Vadis,* and *The Brave Bulls;* the fawn in *The Yearling*—these are players that the camera can uniquely present on the screen.

A school of directors, led by the late Robert J. Flaherty, has specialized in making movies of real-life situations, using non-professional native actors. Flaherty's *Nanook of the North* (1923), which deals with the life of Eskimos, was the first of these realistic pictures. Other films made by Flaherty are *Moana of the South Seas* (1926), picturing life in the Samoan Islands; *Man of Aran* (1934), dealing with the island people of one of the Channel Isles; and *Louisiana Story* (1948), a story of the oil industry in the bayou country. In each of these, the director simply selected persons found on the spot. The use of non-professional actors in factual films is possible because there is usually not much plot or complex character development in them. The director can dramatize settings and locales. He can be a "poet with a camera."

However, for purposes of the popular photoplay, good actors are indeed necessary.

Who is or was the greatest of screen actors? When this question was asked of 200 old-timers around Hollywood studios, some mentioned John or Lionel Barrymore, Wallace Beery, and other favorites whose performances made movie history. But most answers were in accord with what most critics and historians of the motion picture would probably say: Charles Chaplin. Chaplin's pictures touched the hearts of many millions. He became a worldwide symbol of "the little man." When *City Lights* (1931) was re-issued after twenty years, *Time* magazine spoke of it as a picture that would endure as long as films are shown.

Later Chaplin films, like *Modern Times* (1936), *The Great Dictator* (1940), *Monsieur Verdoux* (1947), and *Limelight* (1952), were greeted with serious critical consideration. Working to develop each film personally, from inception to finished product, Chaplin has controlled each detail and is therefore entirely responsible for the quality of the work he has done. His work has probably been subjected to more detailed examination by critics than the work of any other film artist with the possible exception of D. W. Griffith.

Who are other actors who might be called great? Among the most creative individuals in the business of making films are Sir Laurence Olivier and Orson Welles. Both of these men are more than film actors. Each has succeeded on the stage. Each has become a director and producer of his own films. Each possesses originality of a high order.

Olivier is one of the most distinguished actors on the contemporary stage. He has played a great variety of roles, each requiring him to become something other than himself. In Hollywood, which tends to type its stars so that the public will know what to expect, Olivier became a somewhat gloomy hero in *Wuthering Heights* (1939) and *Rebecca* (1940). However, in Britain, his greatest success has been in such varied roles as *Henry V* (1946) and *Hamlet* (1948). Both of these films were directed by Olivier. When he was in a scene, his cameraman took over as director. These Shakespearean films were artistic triumphs, proving once and for all that Shakespeare, intelligently brought to the screen, is the greatest of scenarists. If Olivier were to retire from motion-picture acting at this point, his greatness would be assured. His screen versions of *Henry V, Hamlet,* and *Richard III* will remain as milestones in film history.

Orson Welles, before he turned to film-making, had established himself as a star in both theater and radio. His Mercury Theater troupe produced many significant hits, including *Julius Caesar* in modern dress. His radio dramatization of *Invasion from Mars,* based on H. G. Wells' *The War of the Worlds,* set off a public panic. Then, at the age of twenty-five, he wrote, directed, produced, and played the lead in *Citizen Kane* (1941), a work of film art. Although this picture was not widely distributed, it was considered by critics to be a remarkable achievement in many ways. The story it told, of the rise to power of an ambitious young publisher with high ideals and of the gradual tarnishing of those ideals, was full of social meaning. The acting was considered excellent. The technical innovations, relating to lighting, set design, and photography, were hailed by other studio-workers as revolutionary.

Welles followed this success with another successful film, *Magnificent Ambersons* (1942), which he directed but in which he did not act. This picture, adapted from a Booth

Tarkington novel, reaffirmed his reputation for keen understanding of photoplay art. Some other films directed and acted in by Welles are *The Stranger* (1946), *The Lady from Shanghai* (1948), *Macbeth* (1948), and *Othello* (1952). As an actor he has appeared in such other films as *Jane Eyre* (1944), *Prince of Foxes* (1949), and *The Third Man* (1950).

Not every critic considers Welles as well-suited for films as for other media. His voice and bearing are sometimes overtheatrical, lacking in the restraint that marks the most effective screen appearances. However, Welles is a man with years of service yet ahead of him. The fact that he combines immense creativity with a genius for getting interesting work accomplished marks him as one of the outstanding film actors of our times.

Which other actors should be named as exceptional among the many fine performers in Hollywood? Older stars, durable men, are Fredric March, Humphrey Bogart, Walter Pidgeon, Edward G. Robinson, and Spencer Tracy. All have received high praise from the critics.

Fredric March began his career on the stage. Following his first appearance in movies in 1929, March rapidly became a box-office attraction. For his work in *Dr. Jekyll and Mr. Hyde* (1932) he won the Academy Award. Other successful pictures of his are *The Barretts of Wimpole Street* (1934), *Anna Karenina* (1935), *A Star Is Born* (1937), *Victory* (1940), *So Ends Our Night* (1941), and *The Best Years of Our Lives* (1946), for which he again won the Academy Award. He has since appeared in *Another Part of the Forest* (1948), *Christopher Columbus* (1949), *Death of a Salesman* (1951), *The Bridges of Toko-Ri* (1954), *Alexander the Great* (1956), and *Man in the Gray Flannel Suit* (1956).

Humphrey Bogart, on the screen since 1932, won the

Academy Award in 1952 for his remarkable performance as a character actor in *The African Queen*.

How Green Was My Valley and *Man Hunt*, both made in 1941, were Walter Pidgeon's most successful early pictures. *Mrs. Miniver* (1942) established him as a highly competent actor, with more than the usual ability to carry a demanding role. In 1949 he appeared in two outstanding pictures, *Command Decision* and *That Forsyte Woman*.

Edward G. Robinson first starred in gangster roles like that of *Little Caesar* (1930). He has appeared in such pictures as *The Sea Wolf* (1941), *The Woman in the Window* (1944), *Our Vines Have Tender Grapes* (1945), *All My Sons* (1948), *Night Has a Thousand Eyes* (1948), and *House of Strangers* (1949). Robinson's skill in character portrayal has made him one of the few stars whose range of roles is apparently unlimited.

Spencer Tracy, whose acting won the Academy Award for two successive years with *Captains Courageous* (1937) and *Boys Town* (1938), is another such versatile star. *Fury* (1936), with a social theme, portrayed Tracy as the victim of a lynch-mad mob. Since then, he has varied his roles widely.

Other men whose acting has been less consistently admired than that of the preceding group and yet who are outstanding actors are Gary Cooper, Clark Gable, Tyrone Power, Robert Taylor, and John Wayne. They are competent, popular players of great box-office value.

Born in Montana, Gary Cooper brought his lanky good looks to Hollywood in the early twenties, playing his first leading role in *The Winning of Barbara Worth* (1926). Rising quickly to stardom, Cooper played in many pictures, including such successes as *Farewell to Arms* (1932), with Helen Hayes, and *Mr. Deeds Goes to Town* (1936). For his acting in *Sergeant York* (1941), he won the Academy Award of that year. Among his more notable later pictures are *Task Force* (1949) and *High Noon* (1952).

Clark Gable seemed most successful as a gangster or tough type until he appeared with Claudette Colbert in Frank Capra's *It Happened One Night* (1932), a romantic comedy that won Academy Awards for both the stars and the director. Gable achieved great success also in *Mutiny on the Bounty* (1935) and *Gone With the Wind* (1939).

Tyrone Power came to stardom over night with *The Lloyds of London* (1936) and has continued to be highly popular. He has appeared in many pictures of a costume or historical type, such as *Blood and Sand* (1941), *The Black Swan* (1942), and *Prince of Foxes* (1950).

Robert Taylor emerged as a star at the same time, appearing with Greta Garbo in *Camille* (1936), which has been revived as a classic in 1955. Taylor has appeared in many box-office successes, including *Quo Vadis* (1951), *Ivanhoe* (1952), *Knights of the Round Table* (1954), and *Quentin Durward* (1955).

John Wayne is unusual in many ways. Born Marion Michael Morrison, at Winterset, Iowa, he worked up in the motion-picture industry from property man to actor. He ranks near the top in box-office appeal. He was directed by John Ford in the successful *Stage Coach* (1939). Since that time, he has played a great variety of ruggedly virile roles, with increasing popular success. In 1948, he was starred in two of the best westerns ever made, *Fort Apache* and *Red River*. He has since been directed by Ford in *She Wore a Yellow Ribbon* (1949), *The Quiet Man* (1952), and *The Searchers* (1956).

Any list of established male stars should include also

Henry Fonda, Cary Grant, James Mason, Ray Milland, James Stewart, and William Holden.

Among the newer movie stars, Gregory Peck is one who stands out. Peck attended the University of California at Los Angeles, where he studied dramatics. He appeared in several New York stage productions, none of which was a hit. He has had a variety of movie roles in *The Yearling* (1946), *Gentleman's Agreement* (1947), *The Paradine Case* (1948), *Twelve O'Clock High* (1950), *David and Bathsheba* (1951), *Roman Holiday* (1953), *Man in the Gray Flannel Suit* (1956), and *Moby Dick* (1956).

Montgomery Clift, another comparative newcomer, shows promise of joining the ranks of distinguished actors. Two of his best roles have been those he played in *The Heiress* (1949) and *A Place in the Sun* (1951).

Marlon Brando has come to the fore with an "Oscar" for his performance in *On the Waterfront*. He also made a hit as Mark Antony in *Julius Caesar*.

Among long-lasting movie actors are those who specialize in portraying many kinds of character roles. Such an actor is Barry Fitzgerald. He came to the movies from The Abbey Theater Players of Dublin, Ireland. Among his early film successes were *The Plough and the Stars* (1936) and *How Green Was My Valley* (1941). As the aging priest in *Going My Way* (1944), he won that year's Academy Award as best supporting actor. He has done even better in *The Quiet Man* (1952).

Perhaps no actor on the screen has played a greater variety of roles than Charles Laughton. Since earning the Academy Award for his performance in *The Private Life of Henry VIII* (1933), he has played in *Mutiny on the Bounty* (1935), *Ruggles of Red Gap* (1935), *Hunchback of Notre Dame*

(1939), *Bagdad on the Subway* (1952), and other fine pictures.

Sir Ralph Richardson appeared in *Anna Karenina* (1948), *The Heiress* (1949), and *The Fallen Idol* (1949). Clifton Webb, as the eccentric but resourceful and witty Mr. Belvedere in *Sitting Pretty,* created a character whose adventures continued in follow-up films. In 1950 he appeared in *Cheaper by the Dozen.*

Other character actors on the screen have been Edward Arnold, Edmund Gwenn, Sir Cedric Hardwicke, Adolphe Menjou, Thomas Mitchell, and Edmond O'Brien. Bing Crosby's performance in *The Country Girl* (1954) won wide acclaim and established him as a character actor as well as a popular comedian and singer. Alec Guiness has a growing reputation as a character actor.

Screen Actresses

Who is or was the greatest screen actress? Some of the old-timers mention Marie Dressler, who was teamed with Wallace Beery, but most people name Greta Garbo as the best actress. Although she has not made a motion picture for a number of years, Garbo, as she was familiarly known at the height of her fame, remains as perhaps the most romantic yet seriously-considered among the many women who have achieved movie stardom.

Garbo came to the United States in the early twenties as the protege of the Swedish director, Mauritz Stiller. In 1926, with her first American film, *The Torrent,* she became a top romantic star. Much was written about the source of her "allure." Garbo's face, with its high cheek-bones and deep-set eyes, was especially suited to appearance before the camera. She became a symbol of mystery, in part because of her insistence upon absolute privacy off the screen.

Garbo appeared notably in *Flesh and the Devil* (1927), *A Woman of Affairs* (1929), *Anna Christie* (1930), *Queen Christina* (1933), *Anna Karenina* (1935), *Camille* (1936), and *Ninotchka* (1939).

Bette Davis has won the Academy Award twice, in 1935 for *Dangerous* and in 1938 for *Jezebel*. She became a star with her appearance in *Of Human Bondage* (1934), an "unsympathetic" part which seems to have turned her toward the selection of roles which are not usually thought of as romantic. Examples are *The Old Maid* (1939), *The Letter* (1940), *The Little Foxes* (1941), *Now, Voyager* (1942), *A Stolen Life* (1946), and *Beyond the Forest* (1949). Occasionally Miss Davis has attempted comedy roles. One of her most successful was in *June Bride* (1948).

Greer Garson, an English actress, became well known with her performance in *Good-bye Mr. Chips* (1939), in which Robert Donat played the title role with extraordinary success. She succeeded in winning the Academy Award for her acting in *Mrs. Miniver* (1942). Since then, she has appeared in pictures as varied as *Madame Curie* (1943), *Julia Misbehaves* (1948), *That Forsyte Woman* (1949), and *Julius Caesar* (1953). Miss Garson possesses a beautiful speaking voice, in addition to having the kind of beauty which Technicolor was created to record.

Among the many other fine actresses, Claudette Colbert, Irene Dunne, Katharine Hepburn, Rosalind Russell, and Loretta Young have long maintained stardom.

Claudette Colbert began her screen stardom when she appeared with Fredric March in *Manslaughter* in 1930, and maintained it in such DeMille productions as *Sign of the Cross* (1932) and *Cleopatra* (1934); but her real popularity dates from 1934, when she and Clark Gable both won Academy Awards in *It Happened One Night*. In that same year,

Miss Colbert starred in a tragic social drama entitled *Imitation of Life*. Thus she proved she could play both comic and tragic roles. Subsequently she was seen in *The Egg and I* (1947), *Bride for Sale* (1949), and *Three Came Home* (1950).

During her long career, Irene Dunne has likewise played a variety of roles. Her first notable success was in *Cimarron* (1931), followed by *Back Street* (1932), *Show Boat* (1936), *The Awful Truth* (1937), *My Favorite Wife* (1940), and *The White Cliffs of Dover* (1944). Later successes were *Anna and the King of Siam* (1946), *Life With Father* (1946), and *I Remember Mama* (1948).

Katharine Hepburn received the Academy Award for her acting in *Morning Glory* (1932), following which she appeared in *Little Women* (1933), *Stage Door* (1937), and *The Philadelphia Story* (1940). More recently she has been seen in *Sea of Grass* (1947), *State of the Union* (1948), *Adam's Rib* (1949), and *The African Queen* (1952).

Rosalind Russell's first notable starring role was in *Craig's Wife* (1936), following which she appeared in *The Women* (1939), *His Girl Friday* (1939), *My Sister Eileen* (1942), *Sister Kenny* (1946), *Mourning Becomes Electra* (1948), *A Woman of Distinction* (1950), and *Picnic* (1956).

Loretta Young, who made her screen debut when she was fifteen, won the Academy Award in 1947 for her acting in *The Farmer's Daughter*. Other pictures in which she has appeared include *Rachel and the Stranger* (1948), *Mother Is a Freshman* (1949), *Come to the Stable* (1949), and *Key to the City* (1950).

Other leading actresses of long standing on the screen are Marlene Dietrich, Hedy Lamarr, Myrna Loy, and Barbara Stanwyck.

Marlene Dietrich was imported as a German Garbo. She

had played in many successful foreign movies. As directed by Joseph von Sternberg, Miss Dietrich became a synonym for glamor in such pictures as *Shanghai Express* (1932) and *The Song of Songs* (1933). She played supporting roles with great distinction in *A Foreign Affair* (1948) and *Stage Fright* (1950).

Hedy Lamarr was another importation. Born in Vienna, Miss Lamarr began her career in Austrian studios as a script girl. Since coming to this country, she has specialized in roles capitalizing upon her beauty, beginning with such pictures as *Algiers* (1938) and *White Cargo* (1942). She was starred in the 1949 DeMille production, *Samson and Delilah*.

Myrna Loy began her film career in roles that seemed to type her as an Oriental menace. Then the success of *The Thin Man* (1934) with William Powell widened her scope to include comedy leads. Miss Loy has been seen in *The Bachelor and the Bobby-Soxer* (1947), *Mr. Blandings Builds His Dream House* (1948), and *Cheaper by the Dozen* (1950).

Barbara Stanwyck has been successful in *The Bitter Tea of General Yen* (1933), *Golden Boy* (1939), *The Lady Eve* (1941), *Double Indemnity* (1944), *The Two Mrs. Carrolls* (1947), *B. F.'s Daughter* (1948), *East Side, West Side* (1948), *Thelma Jordan* (1950), and a number of recent films.

Younger winners of Academy Awards for acting include Olivia deHavilland, Joan Fontaine, Jennifer Jones, Vivien Leigh, Jane Wyman, Audrey Hepburn, and Grace Kelly.

Miss deHavilland, who won awards for *To Each His Own* (1947) and *The Heiress* (1949), and Joan Fontaine, who won hers for *Suspicion* (1941), are sisters. They were born in Tokyo, where their father was representing an American firm, and were brought up in California. Olivia's chance at the movies came while she was serving as understudy in a

Hollywood Bowl production of *A Midsummer Night's Dream* and caught the eye of the great German director, Max Reinhardt, who cast her in the screen version of that Shakespearean play. Her appearance as Melanie in *Gone With the Wind* (1939) showed that she could play non-romantic parts. She gained stature in *The Dark Mirror* (1946), *The Snake Pit* (1948), and *The Heiress* (1949).

Joan Fontaine, whose acting has also been widely applauded, is best known for her roles in *Rebecca* (1940), *Jane Eyre* (1944), *Ivy* (1947), *The Emperor Waltz* (1948), and *Ivanhoe* (1952). While her style of acting is not so dramatic as her sister's, Miss Fontaine is remarkable for ability to carry difficult parts.

The Song of Bernadette (1944) made a star of Jennifer Jones and brought her an Academy Award. She has been successful in *Cluny Brown* (1946), *Duel in the Sun* (1947), *Madame Bovary* (1949), and *Portrait of Jennie* (1949). Her recent films include *Good Morning, Miss Dove* and *Love Is a Many-Splendored Thing*. She has just been starred in a new version of *The Barretts of Wimpole Street*.

Vivien Leigh, as Scarlett O'Hara in *Gone With the Wind* (1939), won an Academy Award with one of the most memorable characterizations in movie history. In *That Hamilton Woman* (1941), *Caesar and Cleopatra* (1945), *Anna Karenina* (1948), and *Streetcar Named Desire* (1952), Miss Leigh, who is married to Sir Laurence Olivier, continued her screen work. *Streetcar* brought her a second Academy Award.

Jane Wyman won her Academy Award for her appealing performance as a deaf mute in *Johnny Belinda* (1948). Earlier she had appeared in *The Yearling* (1946). More recently she made a hit in *Magnificent Obsession* (1954).

Among actresses unusually capable of carrying supporting

roles in character parts have been Judith Anderson, Ethel Barrymore, Elsa Lanchester, and Edna May Oliver.

Judith Anderson has appeared in *Rebecca* (1940), *Specter of the Rose* (1946), and *Pursued* (1947), among many other films.

Ethel Barrymore, long a stage star, appeared with her two brothers in *Rasputin and the Empress* in 1932, after which she refused to make another film appearance until she was persuaded to join the cast of *None But the Lonely Heart* (1944), for which she received the Academy Award as supporting actress. After that picture, she appeared in a number of others, including *The Spiral Staircase* (1946), *The Paradine Case* (1948), and *Pinky* (1949).

Elsa Lanchester, originally a stage player, specializes in comic roles of the sort seen in *The Razor's Edge* (1946), *The Big Clock* (1949), *Come to the Stable* (1949), *The Inspector General* (1949), and *The Glass Slipper* (1955). An actress with undoubted talent, married to Charles Laughton, Miss Lanchester brightens any film in which she appears.

Countless pictures gained strength from the appearance of the late Edna May Oliver. She made a marvelous Ugly Duchess in *Alice in Wonderland* (1933) and was a perfect Betsey Trotwood in *David Copperfield* (1935). One of her best roles was the nurse in *Romeo and Juliet* (1936). She also appeared as Lady Catherine de Burgh in *Pride and Prejudice* (1940).

Out of the thousands of actors and actresses who have appeared on the screen, we have mentioned only a limited number. The screen needs great actors and actresses of all sorts. A few, as we have seen, have made screen history.

Suggested Activities

1. Choose one of the actors or actresses discussed in this chapter as the subject of a more detailed biographical report. Include in your research the location of critical comments on the acting of the star on whom you are reporting.

2. What kind of acting do you think requires the greatest skill: comic, romantic, tragic, "dramatic," or "character" acting? Justify your answer.

3. Examine stories about popular actors or actresses in several copies of movie magazines. What kinds of information do the magazine writers seem to think will prove most interesting to readers?

4. Examine several different Hollywood gossip columns. Can you tell from your examination which types of news the columnists seem to prefer? To what extent do such columns serve as publicity channels for information about forthcoming productions? What proportion of the columns you surveyed are devoted to gossip about the personal lives of Hollywood personalities? How do you account for the popularity of such columns?

5. What do you know about "fan clubs"? Report on your personal experiences, if any, with such clubs. Write to several studios for information about their fan clubs for popular stars.

6. Report on your personal preferences among film actors and actresses. Report on your own experiences as a "fan." How have your preferences changed since you first had favorites among the movie stars? Have you ever collected pictures of your favorites? Made scrap-books? Written "fan" letters? Who are your favorite stars today? Why? Are they listed in *Who's Who in America*?

11

Standards of Cinematography

HAVE YOU seen the initials "A.S.C." after the name of the movie cameraman in the credit titles at the beginning of a photoplay? It means that the cameraman has achieved sufficient technical proficiency to be admitted to the American Society of Cinematographers.

How can one achieve such proficiency? The best way for a beginner to study the elements of cinematography is to spend a year or two as an assistant in one of the big Hollywood film laboratories. There the apprentice cameraman can learn the basic principles of the physics and chemistry of photography. Later, by becoming a member of a camera crew and helping to move cinematographic equipment around, he can become familiar with the various camera set-ups and the mechanics of motion-picture photography. Gradually he can learn how to use the many types of cameras and lenses. He must become expert in the use of filters, gauzes, perambulators, rolling tripods, cranes, booms, dollies, transparencies, reflectors, spotlights, flood lights, light meters, and devices for special effects. The accessories for controlling the quality and quantity of light on a movie set are numerous and complex.

A good cinematographer is essential to the making of a

photoplay. Henry Hathaway, one of the best Hollywood directors, once said: "All I need is a good script and Charlie Lang for my cameraman." Although called a cameraman, the director of photography on a movie stage does not personally handle the cameras and lights. His assistants operate the cameras, accessories, and lighting equipment. He personally works closely with the director. If he is a cooperative person and enjoys working with others, his partnership with the director can be a real one. He must translate the wishes of the director into precise directions of his own. His camera crew must work quickly and smoothly under his direction to secure the right mood and atmosphere for each scene.

Not all members of the A.S.C. are sufficiently versatile to handle the whole range of camera effects, from scenes of mass action to the most intimate close-ups in color. Some cameramen are particularly skillful in solving problems of photography with which the producer and director may be faced. The problem may be to make an actress who is young and glamorous look like an old lady at the end of the story. Or it may be to keep an aging actor looking like a young man. A devoted cameraman can be of great help to a star as well as to a director. Greta Garbo, in her long career at the M-G-M studio, insisted on having Bill Daniels as her cameraman.

The cinematographer can sometimes secure important effects by clever camera tricks. The camera can shock us or make us laugh. It can convey the spirit of outdoor melodrama even though the scene is made inside a studio. In general, cameramen flood a stage with bright lighting for scenes of comedy, and they keep the stage shadowed with somber lighting for serious or tragic scenes.

A good photoplay reveals skill in the dramatic use of light and shadow for every bit of action. No matter how difficult the camera angle, the camera must provide the effect that the director needs. In competent hands, the camera conveys mental images to the movie audience by helping to create dramatic moods. Hence, unless the photographer understands the emotional values of light, shadow, and color, he cannot see eye to eye with the director.

With the sharp upward trend in the percentage of films photographed in Technicolor, Eastman Color, Anscocolor, and other processes, the cameraman must fully understand the psychology of color. Color contributes important emotional values to settings, costumes, props, and facial makeup. Color elements are emphasized or toned down by means of color filters to secure effective stage pictures. For example, blues and greens may be emphasized to suggest calmness and coolness. Reds and yellows may be used to intensify scenes of excitement.

Directors of photography aim for cinematic rhythm and pleasing pictorial composition. Above all, they must secure continuous mobility in their cinematography. Cameramen who win "Oscars" in the annual Academy Awards are masters of flexibility and fluidity of composition. If a cameraman forgets that a movie must move and that a camera must contribute all it can to a continuous narrative flow, he is not living up to his responsibility. Every foot of film must either advance the plot or comment on character.

If a photoplay cameraman pauses for isolated artistic effects—which may in themselves be excellent examples of photography but are unnecessary to the development of the story—his appeal is to a limited audience. In the small, high-class theaters known as "art houses," such examples of pictorial beauty may appeal to special audiences; but most people do not go to movies to see photography for its own sake. It may be effective to focus the camera for a moment on mountain scenery or on a piece of newspaper blowing along the gutter if this keeps the story moving, but not if it slows up the tempo for the sake of what is merely an interesting shot. The consuming interest of the public is in stories. The photography must therefore be a means of story-telling rather than an end in itself.

You may be one of those who enjoy photography so much that you wish to see movies in which the effects are those of a poet with a camera, but most people prefer straight lines of narrative on the screen. Audiences tend to become bored when the picture deviates from the story to become lyrical and descriptive. This is not to say that a picture should avoid special effects. For example, in *Samson and Delilah,* DeMille began with effects of cosmic space and a revolving globe to create the effect of global significance in his opening commentary.

One of the most difficult but important types of cinematic effect lies in the photography of dancing. *An American in Paris* showed what brilliant, kaleidoscopic effects an imaginative producer and cameraman can get in ballet scenes. Only skillful craftsmen can catch the right tempo of dialog while characters are dancing and speaking their lines at the same time. This requires a strong sense of cinematic rhythm. The cameraman as well as the sound engineer must help secure the right effect for each line.

The cameraman must realize that photography of motion is closely related to the arts of music and the dance. Every maximum cinematic effect, whether of normal motion, fast motion, or slow motion, must be photographed with musical cadence as part of an orchestration of continuous rhythm.

In spite of the complexity of the work of the cinematographer, the total effect of his camera language must be to tell a story with utmost simplicity, naturalness, and economy of means. The camera must be terse and concise. The best cameraman is one who says the most in the shortest possible time. He helps the director tell his story in quick strokes which fascinate us. For the screen must continuously hold our attention, whether the scene be intimate or spectacular.

Suggested Activities

1. What photoplays have you seen that are strikingly photographed? What kinds of scenes may depend for their effect mainly on camera work? What makes a photograph good? What is composition? What is contrast? What is a highlight? What is pictorial rhythm?

2. The next time you see a movie, sit through it twice. The second time imagine you are the cameraman and try to answer for yourself why the camera was located where it was for various shots.

3. Some pictures list among their credits a cameraman for "special effects." What is meant by this? What is gained by inserting such effects? Can you give an example and tell why the director or producer considered this necessary?

4. In reference books like *Motion Picture and Television Almanac* and *The Film Daily Year Book,* find out what cameramen have won Academy Awards since 1955.

12

Notable Cinematographers

WE HAVE seen that the cameraman, or cinematographer, is a key figure in the actual filming of the motion picture. Upon his technical knowledge of lenses and exposures and lighting methods depends the over-all pictorial quality of the film. The American Society of Cinematographers, with about 200 members, comprises the leaders of the profession. They try to make a photoplay a thing of beauty rather than simply a commonplace report of what the camera saw.

Great directors work closely with their cameramen and even educate them, as did Griffith. Photographers like to work with John Ford, for example, because he is noted for his fine sense of pictorial composition. Some cameramen are outstanding for their ability to sharpen dramatic effects by strong contrasts of light and shadow; others for their ability to capture the scope of outdoor landscape. Technicolor brought with it experts in color photography. CinemaScope brought experts in panoramic effects.

Cameramen who become experts usually are men who have spent long years meeting and solving numerous technical problems that are presented in making pictures. Thus the leaders in the cinematographic profession are, as a rule, old-timers. One of the outstanding experts in the field is Arthur Miller, sometimes referred to by his associates as "the master." Miller has won the Academy Award for photography three times, with *How Green Was My Valley* (1941), *The Song of Bernadette* (1943), and *Anna and the King of Siam* (1946).

Charles Rosher and Karl Struss won the first Academy Awards for photography in 1928 with their filming of F. W. Murnau's *Sunrise*. Their work is notable for mood and lighting. James Wong Howe is another noted cameraman, with such pictures to his credit as *Algiers* (1938), *King's Row* (1941), and *The Rose Tattoo* (1955). Another highly competent photographer is Gregg Toland, whose work includes some of the most beautifully filmed pictures ever made, *The Grapes of Wrath* (1940), *The Long Voyage Home* (1940), *Citizen Kane* (1941), and *The Best Years of Our Lives* (1946).

Two younger men who have made their mark recently are Gabriel Figueroa and Robert Krasker. Figueroa, a Mexican cameraman, filmed *The Fugitive* (1947) for John Ford and made *The Pearl* (1948) as both director and cameraman. Krasker, an Englishman, did *Henry V* (1946), *Odd Man Out* (1947), and *The Third Man* (1950). His color photography in *Henry V* was considered to have reached a new high for that type of work. In *The Third Man,* Krasker proved himself a master of mood and lighting. The shot of the villain's fingers groping through the sewer grating will probably never be forgotten by anyone who saw it.

Academy Awards for Cinematography

1928: Charles Rosher and Karl Struss, *Sunrise*.
1929: Clyde De Vinna, *White Shadows in the South Seas*.

1930: Willard Van Der Veer and Joseph T. Rucker, *With Byrd at the South Pole.*
1931: Floyd Crosby, *Tabu.*
1932: Lee Garmes, *Shanghai Express.*
1933: Charles Bryant Lang, Jr., *A Farewell to Arms.*
1934: Victor Milner, *Cleopatra.*
1935: Hal Mohr, *A Midsummer Night's Dream.*
1936: Tony Gaudio, *Anthony Adverse.*
1937: Karl Freund, *The Good Earth.*
1938: Joseph Ruttenberg, *The Great Waltz.*
1939: Black-and-white: Gregg Toland, *Wuthering Heights.*
Color: Ernest Haller and Ray Rennahan, *Gone With the Wind.*
1940: Black-and-white: George Barnes, *Rebecca.*
Color: George Perrinal, *The Thief of Bagdad.*
1941: Black-and-white: Arthur Miller, *How Green Was My Valley.*
Color: Ernest Palmer and Ray Rennahan, *Blood and Sand.*
1942: Black-and-white: Joseph Ruttenberg, *Mrs. Miniver.*
Color: Leon Shamroy, *The Black Swan.*
1943: Black-and-white: Arthur Miller, *The Song of Bernadette.*
Color: Hal Mohr and W. Howard Greene, *The Phantom of the Opera.*
1944: Black-and-white: Joseph La Shelle, *Laura.*
Color: Leon Shamroy, *Wilson.*
1945: Black-and-white: Harry Stradling, *The Picture of Dorian Gray.*
Color: Leon Shamroy, *Leave Her to Heaven.*
1946: Black-and-white: Arthur Miller, *Anna and the King of Siam.*

Color: Charles Rosher, Leonard Smith, and Arthur Arling, *The Yearling.*
1947: Black-and-white: Guy Green, *Great Expectations.*
Color: Jack Cardiff, *Black Narcissus.*
1948: Black-and-white: William Daniels, *The Naked City.*
Color: Joseph Valentine, William V. Skall, and Winton Hoch, *Joan of Arc.*
1949: Black-and-white: Paul C. Vogel, *Battleground.*
Color: Winton Hoch, *She Wore a Yellow Ribbon.*
1950: Black-and-white: Robert Krasker, *The Third Man.*
Color: Robert Surtees, *King Solomon's Mines.*
1951: Black-and-white: William C. Mellor, *A Place in the Sun.*
Color: Alfred Gilks and John Alton, *An American in Paris.*
1952: Black-and-white: Robert Surtees, *The Bad and the Beautiful.*
Color: Winton Hoch and Archie Stout, *The Quiet Man.*
1953: Black-and-white: Burnett Guffey, *From Here to Eternity.*
Color: Loyal Griggs, *Shane.*
1954: Black-and-white: Boris Kaufman, *On the Waterfront.*
Color: Milton Krasner, *Three Coins in the Fountain.*
1955: Black-and-white: James Wong Howe, *The Rose Tattoo.*
Color: Robert Burks, *To Catch a Thief.*

In this roster of awards you will note that Winton Hoch, Arthur Miller, and Leon Shamroy are three-time winners of highest honors for cinematography and that the following are two-time winners: Charles Rosher, Joseph Ruttenburg, Ray Rennahan, Hal Mohr, and Robert Surtees. You will note that

Winton Hoch and Leon Shamroy excel in color cinematography and that Arthur Miller excels in black-and-white.

Knowing something about what characterizes good cinematography and becoming acquainted with the names of certain of the outstanding men in the field should contribute to a fuller appreciation of a good photoplay.

Suggested Activities

1. Choose one of the outstanding motion pictures listed in this chapter and look up three or four reviews of it. How many of these reviews include comment on the photography? What points did these comments make?

(Your public library can help you locate older reviews.)

2. Have you seen revivals of any of the outstanding films listed in this chapter? Do you recall from any of them scenes that have remained vivid to you over several years? Try to analyze the reasons for your remembering such scenes as you may recall. To what extent do you think the art of cinematography may have been involved in making a scene memorable?

3. Do you agree or disagree with any of the recent awards? Give your reasons.

4. Choose a scene from some story that is available to the entire class. Prepare a camera script for the scene, indicating when you would use long shots, when close-ups, etc. Compare your script with those of other students in the class.

13

Standards of Photoplay Editing

EVEN THOUGH a photoplay may have the advantages of a good story, good direction, good cinematography, and good performances, it may be handicapped by poor editing, or "cutting." The all-important quality of dramatic excitement in a film depends, in the last analysis, on the skill with which the editor handles the intimate details of filmic continuity.

Indeed, without the services of a keen, watchful, thoughtful, and creative editor, many of the best effects planned by the director may fall flat. Into the editor's lap falls the job of deciding just how long or short each shot should be, how to put together the best footage for maximum audience impact, how to make the finished production flow along as clearly, smoothly, and pleasingly as possible.

To make the relationships between the many shots from all sorts of angles so clear that the meaning of every action and reaction is unmistakable requires craftsmanship of such a high order that producers and directors sometimes do their own editing. During the final stages of production, they closely supervise the work of the cutter. Although editors' names appear in small type on the screen, good editors are among the most highly paid workers in a movie studio.

In the early stages of a production, as the daily "rushes" come from the laboratory, the cutter's work is largely mechanical. As the length of the footage grows from day to day, the work becomes more creative. The business of cutting and putting together the thousands of tiny bits of film out of which the mosaic is fashioned requires a thorough understanding of the psychological elements which go into the making of a satisfying picture. The cutter knows just where quick cutting from shot to shot will create the necessary mood of excitement, where sustaining the action with a longer cut will create dignity, where sudden change will create shock, where a rhythmic crescendo of shorter and shorter cuts will create the effect of climax.

From the great procession of long, medium, and close shots, and from the multiplicity of angles used by the director in striving to get the most effective scenes, the cutter must choose whatever seems most logical and appropriate for the unfolding of the story. At his command the movie editor has various transitional devices, which serve as filmic punctuation—dissolves, fade-ins, fade-outs, iris-ins, iris-outs, lap dissolves, montages, and the carefully measured cuts of parallel action. To speed up the story he may often use simple cuts from scene to scene, so long as the meaning is clear. These devices are defined in the glossary in Chapter 17.

Long experience has taught movie-makers what basic patterns or arrangements of shots are most effective on the screen. The standard procedure is to begin a scene with a long shot, so as to establish the locale or setting of the action, and then to follow with medium shots before using close shots. However, this is only a general rule. Each film, like each stage-play or novel or short-story, is unique. The story-teller has the right to tell his story in his own way. In showmanship there are no rules except that the showman must please his audience.

Naturally the editor must bear in mind that audiences want to know where, when, who, what, how, and why—as soon as possible—once they begin to look at a picture; but there are many roads that lead to the same goals in answering questions which naturally arise in the minds of audiences. For example, an opening sequence may show us, in a series of dissolves, first the rooftops of Paris as they are today, then a certain street in Paris, then a house on that street, then a room in that house, and finally a man brushing his hair before a mirror in that room. Without a word being spoken, but with a musical underscoring that creates the proper mood, we are told that a young Parisian is about to go out for the evening. We are now ready, perhaps, for the scene where boy meets girl.

In studying the construction of photoplays, it is necessary to see films for a second time, or even a third time, in order to observe the sequence of scenes and shots, noting how long each shot is, how the length of shots is varied, how rhythmic action is achieved, how the editor has built suspense. We might call this a study of the grammatical and rhetorical structure of the scenes.

What sequences of action make audiences laugh or cry or cheer or gasp? If the film presents as its central figure a character whom the audience likes, what is the audience reaction if this character is knocked down by a blow? If he remains down, the audience will probably be silent, concerned to find out how badly he is hurt. If he gets up, they may laugh.

Editors need to know what emotional effects will result from juxtapositions of scenes and from timing of shots in a sequence. Cutting an action a second too soon or too late may cause a scene to lose its force. Dramatic effects depend largely on timing, and timing can be spoiled or perfected in the cutting room.

Ever since D. W. Griffith invented the technique of intercutting scenes of parallel action, every editor knows that showing alternate shots of the pursuer and the pursued builds an exciting effect. In westerns, in spy dramas, and in other films showing the chases that movie audiences love, editors can make our hearts beat faster. By means of balanced, rhythmic counterpoint, with shorter and shorter cuts, a crescendo effect is achieved. This is as much a matter of editing as of direction and performance. In more subtle types of action, even the raising of an eyebrow in a close-up, *at the right moment,* may be most significant—for laughter or suspense.

The work of editing is a long and arduous job of seemingly endless re-cutting and re-arranging scenes experimentally until there is not a dull moment in the picture. Important pictures are tried out in sneak previews to test audience reactions, and then re-cut to achieve the best possible theatrical result. A photoplay cannot be made in a vacuum. Nor can it be understood, defined, or evaluated except in terms of its audience. A picture without an audience is not an entertainment. Therefore an editor, like his associates in the studio, must ever strive to please, not himself, but his audience.

In the orchestration of effects which results in the finished film, the composer of the musical score, the conductor of the studio orchestra and the recording staff play vital parts. After the visual continuity has been polished, there remains therefore for the editor the work of adding the sound tracks—music to create and enhance the mood and atmosphere of the story, sound effects to secure needed realism, dubbing-in of improved bits of dialog—assembling and merging sometimes as many as six or eight sound tracks in one track that must be synchronized with the action. To coordinate and dovetail the various sound tracks, each at first on a separate reel, is a matter of great delicacy and technical precision. Sound engineers do wonders for editors, but the responsibility for the finished mosaic is the editor's.

With many resources to aid him in the laboratory, in the engineering department, and in the special-effects department, the editor after all sits alone, or with an assistant cutter, in his cubicle, building the emotional ladders called for by the story. Always mindful of the great audience of millions to whom he hopes the picture will appeal, he measures his success by his ability to create, bit by bit, angle by angle, scene by scene, a cinematic river—sometimes tumbling laughingly, sometimes roaring turbulently, but always holding our attention, always focusing our eyes and ears on the center of interest in the story-line, carrying us forward as rapidly and breathlessly as possible, from crisis to crisis, to the final climax which he hopes will merit our applause.

You can well realize that the physical procedure of cutting a photoplay is a complex one. With a great mass of half-organized filmic material pouring in upon him, the editor must have a very logical mind. As he sits before a compact viewing and sound-reproducing machine called a "Moviola," he sees in miniature all the footage—perhaps ten times as much as will be used in the picture—as it comes from the laboratory. To the jigsaw puzzle of unrelated pieces of film, he must apply himself with concentration, following the shooting script and noting how the director has visualized each scene. He may have to view a thousand feet of film to secure a needed fifty or one hundred feet called for by the scenario.

In dialog sequences, the cutter requires usually only as much footage as is needed for the spoken lines. He shows either the speaker or the listener reacting to the speaker, cutting back and forth with precise timing. If the speaker's words take two seconds, the footage accompanying the words must sometimes run exactly two seconds. Audiences do not like long speeches. Unless the film cuts rapidly to shots showing reactions to the words spoken, interest will lag. In fact, the most telling portions of a film are sometimes not the shots showing a speaker, but the reactions to the words of the speaker. Audiences like to watch actors as they listen and react to spoken words.

The next time you go to a movie, stop up your ears during dialog and watch how the editor cuts rapidly from speaker to speaker. Note also how an off-stage voice is given meaning by the reactions of the listening actor. You will learn how much the meaning of a film depends on the combination of sight and sound if you will first listen to the sound track with your eyes closed and then see the film with your ears stopped.

To identify each scene as the director shoots it, a member of the camera crew holds a slate before the camera at the beginning of each "take." The slate shows the date, the number of the production, the number of the scene, whether it is an interior or an exterior, the number of the take, and the name of the cameraman. This slate, appearing in a close-up at the beginning of each take, and occupying the full frame, enables the editor to identify each piece of film he is working with.

As the shooting progresses, the cutter develops a "work print," so that the producer and director may screen it from day to day in the studio projection room and judge the results they are getting. The work print must be handled with great care. The cutter wears white cotton gloves to avoid getting finger marks on the film. He keeps the cutting room scrupulously clean to avoid scratching the delicate emulsion. The walls and ceiling of his workshop are coated with a non-flaking type of paint. The floors are either enameled or covered with linoleum. The work-table likewise is enameled or linoleum-covered. The table is equipped with a pair of precision-made rewinds, mounted on the right and left sides of the table. These rewinds are revolving spindles with cranks for reeling and unreeling sections of film by hand. As the film is unreeled it passes through a measuring device called a footage counter, which records the length of each piece of film. Fractions of a foot are measured in frames. Since there are 16 frames of 35mm film to a foot, a strip of 2½ feet, for example, is listed as 2 feet, 8 frames. When run through a sound projector or a Moviola, the film has a fixed speed of 24 frames (1½ feet) a second. Thus the exact running time can be determined.

Mechanically, editing is an extremely precise procedure. A few frames too many or too few can spoil the effect of an action or the synchronization of words with lip movements. To do his cutting, the editor does not use a pair of scissors, but a precision-built cutter-and-splicer. This enables him to work with speed and exactness.

After the precious work-print has reached its final stage, the editor writes a cutting continuity. This is a condensed scenario, listing every scene as finally cut, with its exact length in feet and frames, brief descriptions of the action, all the dialog, all the inserts—every foot, shot by shot. In this way the total running time of the picture is determined. The laboratory can now prepare the final negative. After the censorship authorities have approved the cutting continuity and seen a test print, the film is usually given an official seal by the Code Authority and is ready for release.

The editor's final result has been arrived at only after many conferences with those responsible for the production. The work of cutting and polishing each effect has been long and arduous. It has met the critical standards of self-censorship and showmanship. Its fate now lies with the public.

Some studios are famous for remaking films, either re-cutting or re-shooting scenes that prove to be poor when tested in previews. If a picture is an expensive one, involving considerable financial risk, and is found to lack the expected audience appeal, it may still be converted with further revision from a poor or a fair picture to a good one. Sovereignty lies with the great audience, the movie-going public. The editor works to the last minute in his effort to obey the laws of that audience. Eventually the studio feels that it has done all it can to make the picture an appealing one. The laboratory makes hundreds of prints of the film, ships them to the branches, called exchanges, of its distributing organization, and the sales staff offers the picture to theater circuits and theater managers. Meanwhile the advertising, publicity, and exploitation departments of the company launch a nationwide campaign to sell the picture to the public.

The importance of the editor in determining the interest and effectiveness of the final version of a motion picture is thus seen to be very great. Becoming aware of some of the ways in which films are built up out of their many smaller pieces should add to the enjoyment the movie-goer has in appreciating the craftsmanship which goes into the making of a good movie.

Suggested Activities

1. This chapter includes many technical terms that may well be added to the vocabulary you are building out of the study of motion pictures. Check first to find the definitions of these new terms by the way in which they are used. Then turn

to the glossary of terms at the end of this book and verify the meanings.

2. Do you understand why some great directors have insisted upon editing their own films? To what extent may a director still control the editing, even if he does not do it personally?

3. The musical scores for some motion pictures have been truly fine compositions. Some of this music has been recorded and issued for purchase. Can you locate such an album for class listening?

4. Invite an amateur film-maker to demonstrate some of the principles of editing discussed in this chapter. Perhaps he will present a film and discuss the technical aspects of editing by reference to it.

14

What Makes a Photoplay Significant?

HOW SIGNIFICANT can a motion picture be? In these days, following important decisions of the United States Supreme Court, the motion-picture industry is becoming increasingly conscious of its power and of its responsibility for presenting major issues and ideas. If films can enjoy the same freedom of expression as the press, they can be as significant as any other kind of communication. A movie can say something important, just as a book can. Yet until recently, leaders of the film industry were certain that this mass-communication medium should not try to do more than entertain, so far as the general public is concerned.

During the depression of the 1930's, while the United States was undergoing one of its severest tests as a nation, critics of Hollywood were charging that the movies were ignoring social and economic conditions. Instead of trying to help the American people gain an understanding of their problems, the movies—so these critics charged—were busy turning out frivolous and lightweight films, offering the public "escape" from its troubles instead of throwing light on them. What the public wanted, when it bought tickets to the movies, was entertainment. Perhaps it was relief from troubles, or "escape," that the public was seeking. If so, the movies could do much to help. As for setting out to shape public opinion or inform it, well, that was not the business of Hollywood. It wouldn't be good for business; it wouldn't pay.

A great deal has happened since then to change the minds of motion-picture industry executives. Perhaps as important as anything was the truly remarkable way in which Hollywood went all-out during World War II to gather facts and tell the story of the war. Many top directors, along with producers, cameramen, and other technicians, were in the service, concerned with reporting the war. The short documentary films that came out, dealing for example with air battles, as in *Memphis Belle* (1944) and *The Fighting Lady* (1945), were as exciting and absorbing as full-length story-films like *Action on the North Atlantic* (1943), *Thirty Seconds Over Tokyo* (1944), or *The Story of G. I. Joe* (1945). Training films for the various branches of the service were also being produced either in Hollywood or by its personnel. The growth during the war in understanding of the power of the educational film contributed to Hollywood's knowledge of its power. John Huston, for example, was influenced by his wartime movie work for Uncle Sam.

It became apparent that *entertainment* needs a new definition. It must include whatever is of interest to large numbers of people. Serious subjects of social or artistic significance can grip the attention of intelligent movie-goers. If properly exploited, they can do well at the box-office, as proved by the success of *Anything Can Happen, Cyrano de Bergerac, A Place in the Sun, Death of a Salesman, Julius Caesar, Not as a Stranger, Robinson Crusoe, On the Waterfront,* and *War and Peace.* This trend toward the production of significant films is, happily, continuing.

Another factor that has helped change the motion-picture

industry's mind is the phenomenal success in this country of outstanding post-war films from Italy, France, and England. These films have often dealt with themes that Hollywood would have considered sure death at the box-office. Made under adverse conditions, often with inadequate technical assistance and with no regard for the slick finish that characterizes even the cheapest of American productions, such pictures from Italy as *Open City* (1945), *Shoe-Shine* (1947), and *Paisan* (1948), brought the meaning of war close to home. From England, *Henry V* (1946), *Great Expectations* (1947), *Red Shoes* (1948), *Hamlet* (1948), had successes that gave Hollywood something to think about.

A third factor might well relate to the growth of a new kind of public. The literacy of movie-goers, or at least of potential movie-goers, has risen sharply. This is not merely the kind of literacy that means ability to read and write. The quality of best-selling books is distinctly superior to what it was a generation ago. Magazines are much improved, and the stories they use are more intimately related to life. Young persons more and more are staying in school through the twelfth grade; millions are attending college. With the upward trend of secondary and higher education, more people are learning to read good books. More people discuss personal and social problems with understanding than ever before.

In 1947, two films, *Crossfire* and *Gentleman's Agreement,* looked straight at the problem of anti-Semitism in the United States—and were popular successes. *Gentleman's Agreement* won the Academy Award for the best picture of the year. In 1948, *The Search* dealt successfully with the problem of lost children in a war-ravaged Europe. *The Snake Pit,* in which the heroine was a patient in a mental hospital, was a first-rate movie. In 1949, Hollywood produced four films that dealt in various ways with the problem of prejudice against Negroes:

Home of the Brave, Lost Boundaries, Pinky, and *Intruder in the Dust.* These films all dealt with a sociological problem; they made money as well. And they proved, perhaps once and for all, *that motion pictures can have something significant to say.* At first banned in Texas, *Pinky* was given a new birth of freedom by the Supreme Court.

In judging the sociological value of such films, negative standards are not enough for the student of photoplay appreciation. Yet the Production Code Administration of the Hollywood industry applies a system of self-censorship which is purely negative. The administrators of the Code have done an excellent job of supervising the efforts of the studios to keep out of trouble with pressure groups of all sorts. The Code Administration makes sure that no Hollywood film shows disrespect for any nation, race, or religion; that no film ridicules law or justifies brutal revenge; that no film shows methods of vice or crime in detail or in a way that may inspire imitation; that no film shows bad taste in the treatment of gruesomeness; that all films observe the conventions of decency in matters of sex; that expressions of profanity and scenes of excessive drinking are toned down or avoided.

However, the avoidance of bad taste, bad example, slander, or propaganda does not guarantee that a picture is worth while. Such criteria as those once suggested by the Institute for Propaganda Analysis can help to provide a basis for the appreciation of film significance. The Institute paved the way for developing important criteria by pointing out the errors made by many films in implying "that if you catch the criminal, you solve the crime problem; that war and the preparation for war are thrilling, heroic, and glamorous; that the successful culmination of a romance will solve most of the dilemmas of the hero and the heroine; and that the good life is the acquisitive life, with its emphasis on luxury, fine homes, automobiles, evening dress, swank, and suavity."

Positive criteria of social value must consider whether the leading characters in the film have life-problems that are rooted in ideals of devotion to family, community, mankind —or womankind. For example, Humphrey Bogart's performance in John Huston's picture, *The African Queen,* emphasized ideals of service to one's country even though far away in the heart of Africa. Bogart earned the Academy Award as the best screen actor of 1951 not only because of his convincing performance, but because he helped the director portray winning ideals of honesty, courage, self-sacrifice, patriotism, and respect for womanhood.

To be socially significant, a film must present a true picture. It may of course make its comment on significant aspects of life and human development with light touches, as in *The Man in the White Suit,* a charming comedy concerned in part with the problems of daily living. A good film treats *honestly and adequately* the mode of life with which it purports to deal. If it concerns crime problems, it reveals conditions which are at the root of crime problems—clearly indicating that social, economic, and political conditions are potent contributors to the making of a villain. The struggle can well be between the individual and his environment. Problems of unemployment, insecurity, poor housing, slums, lack of vocational education, lack of training in citizenship are intimately bound up with crime. These, as well as the individual, should be dramatized.

In general, to be significant, a film should contribute something to our understanding of ourselves and our surroundings. In judging a film, ask whether it touches life intimately and realistically. Is its appeal personal and vital? Does it illuminate problems of human behavior? Does it stimulate you to try to understand other people, and yourself, better? Does it do these things thrillingly and with touches of beauty? Only then, from the standpoint of an intelligent movie-goer, can it be truly exciting.

Suggested Activities

1. Write a report on "Significant Motion Pictures I Have Seen." Tell how each of these films contributed to your understanding of the world around you.
2. Cooperate in compiling a list of significant films out of the movie experiences of the entire class. Include annotations as to the reason for each motion picture's significance. Post the list for reference on your classroom bulletin board or elsewhere in the school, or offer it for publication in your school newspaper.
3. Try to locate lists of significant films as given by critics of the motion picture. Discuss these lists in class and compare them with the one made by the class itself.

15

How to Become a Better Movie-Goer

TEACHERS GENERALLY have not done much to help educate the movie-goer to become a better consumer. They have thought of the theatrical motion picture as somehow outside their proper area for teaching. In the past this has been due in part to the fact that there has not been much help in this field for teachers and students. Furthermore, teachers have been handicapped by the fact that many students are better acquainted with feature films than are their teachers. Statistics about movie-going reveal that most movie-goers are young people. After persons grow older, they care less about films.

Television is changing all that. Little by little, the movies of the past are being made available for video broadcasting. Movie stars are signing up for productions made especially for television. A large part of the teen-age audience for movies has been captured for television. As a result of this trend, it is suggested by students of motion-picture problems that theatrical photoplays are destined to become fewer and better, with longer runs in selected houses throughout the country. Movie audiences of the more intelligent type are being attracted to the newer programs. Whereas in the recent past, critics have pointed out that movies have tended to cater too much to adolescents, in the future there will be a stratification of movie audiences. Already this trend is established in our larger cities, where specialized movie houses appeal to particular groups of discriminating patrons.

Enterprising producers of movies have come to realize that we have had too many childish movies and that the needs and interests of young people have not always been met. Youth has been "sold short" because its intelligence has been underestimated. Inevitably now better movies are coming to our theaters.

You as a student can become a better movie-goer by reading the many interesting articles about the movies appearing in our national magazines. These articles are indexed regularly in the *Reader's Guide to Periodical Literature,* published by the H. W. Wilson Company and available in nearly all public libraries, as well as in the larger school libraries. Almost every national magazine, from time to time, publishes articles about the movies. Some magazines review movies regularly. These include *Time, The Saturday Review, Newsweek, Look, The New Yorker, Good Housekeeping, McCall's, Woman's Home Companion, Parents' Magazine, Cue, Cosmopolitan,* and *Redbook.* Educational & Recreational Guides, Inc., 10 Brainerd Road, Summit, New Jersey, has published *Photoplay Studies* regularly since 1935.

Most fan papers grow too enthusiastic about almost any picture. Their best value is in providing lively factual information about forthcoming films. Skip the adjectives and get the facts from such magazines.

You can become a better movie-goer also by doing more newspaper reading about films. However, you should not accept as final what any critic says about a movie. Consider whether critics give *reasons* for their opinions. It is sometimes

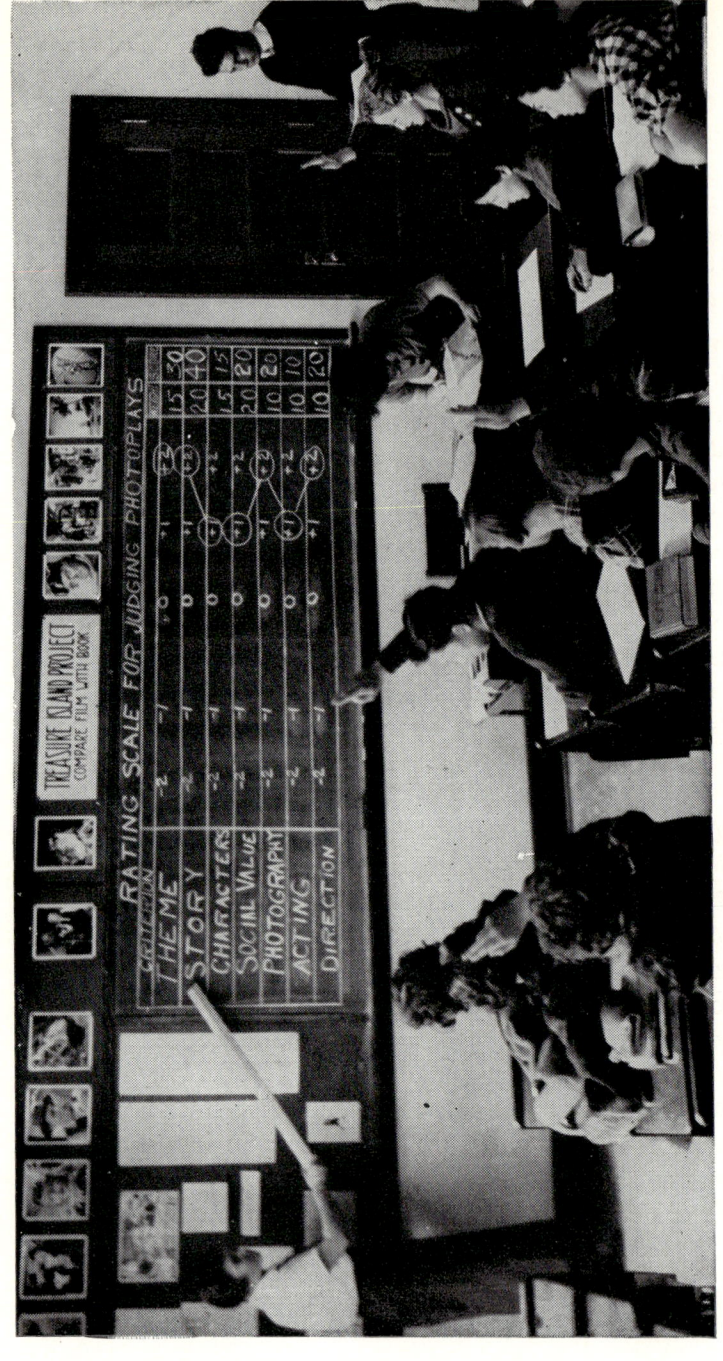

A pioneer class in photoplay appreciation using a rating scale at Weequahic High School, Newark, New Jersey. This school was designated by the New Jersey State Department of Education as an audio-visual demonstration center and awarded a certificate of merit and much valuable equipment.

fun to compare their impressions with your own and with those of other critics. Critics do not agree. They are often wrong. Writing under daily pressure, newspaper critics are not so good as magazine critics. Each critic speaks from his own background and usually reveals only his personal likes and dislikes. No judge of a movie can escape the influence of his background of experience.

The best value you can derive from reading what critics have to say about movies is to get some idea as to the type of film under discussion, and an impression of its story, suspending judgment until you yourself have seen the picture. Most newspapers have motion-picture departments which publicize the story-content of pictures. Some newspapers have able critics, particularly those in the big cities, but you should not be guided so much by the opinions of these critics as by the factual information which they offer.

The most important things to know in shopping for a picture to see are whether it presents a good story and whether it was made by a good director. Although many fine movies are based on original stories, most of the great movies have been based on successful novels and plays. Consider also the reputation of the producer. Of course, the players are important in a photoplay, but the best players and the best director may be handicapped by a poor story. You will never find this out by merely looking at the marquee of the theater for the names of the stars or by reading the advertisements in newspapers and magazines. You must make it your business to get information regarding the content of pictures before laying down your money at the box-office or spending time before a television receiver. This information, coupled with information as to the reputations of those responsible for the production, is your best guide.

Even though you may not be interested in the fact that

TENTATIVE (EXPERIMENTAL) RATING-SCALE FOR JUDGING PHOTOPLAYS AND MEASURING APPRECIATION—GRADES 11 AND 12

Name of Pupil .... Age .... Grade .... Sex .... School .... City ....

Name of Picture .... Producer .... Author .... Director .... Star ....

	−1	0	+1	+2	+3	SCORE	WEIGHT	WEIGHTED SCORE
BASIC THEME........	Lacking	Of Little or No Importance	Timely, Significant	Vitally Important	Momentous, Epical		10	
STORY COMPOSITION......	Incoherent	Possible, but Not Plausible	Rather Logical	Highly Probable	Flawless in Continuity		20	
CHARACTERIZATIONS......	Overdrawn, Unnatural	Rather Stereotyped	Likable	Touching	Genuine		15	
DIALOGUE...........	Trite	Colorless	Rather Witty	Clever	Brilliant		5	
VOICE OF STAR.......	Annoying, Defective	Rather Uncultured	Not Very Noticeable	Effective	Remarkably Versatile		5	
ACTING OF STAR......	Overdone	Obviously Artificial	Casual	Subtle, Charming	Sincere, Life-like		10	
DIRECTION..........	Weak, Dull	Irregular	Smooth	Swift, Convincing	Strikingly Imaginative		10	
PICTORIAL COMPOSITION...	Ugly	Ordinary	Appropriate	Unusual in Photography	Consistently Beautiful		5	
SOCIAL VALUE........	Destructive	Harmless	Wholesome	Commendable	Inspiring to High Ideals		10	
ENJOYMENT..........	Disgusting, Boring	Little or No Interest	Entertaining	Thrilling	Absorbing		10	

TOTAL SCORE........
PERCENTAGE SCORE........

Note: The score which the pupil assigns to each item, multiplied by the weight, gives the weighted score. Highest possible total score is 300. To obtain percentage score, divide total score by 3.

movies shown in theaters are becoming more and more adult in their appeal, you, as a student, should remember that the purpose of high-school education is to convert you from a child to an adult. The authors of this book have a healthy respect for the growing discrimination of high-school students.

Some of the most enterprising schools have equipped themselves to show 16mm versions of older photoplays in their auditoriums. Such schools are preparing to teach units of study in types of the photoplay. Encyclopaedia Britannica Films, Wilmette, Illinois, through its subsidiary, Films Incorporated, is offering an extraordinary array of feature films for use in schools. Included in the list are all the 20th Century-Fox CinemaScope features that are more than a year old, many of the Metro-Goldwyn-Mayer and Warner Brothers features, and a number of independent productions. RKO-Radio Pictures has a 16mm department at 1270 Avenue of the Americas, New York City, which offers most of the older RKO features to schools. Practically all important feature films, except those of Paramount, now become available to schools in 16mm after the theatrical distribution has been completed.

It is now possible for teachers to organize curriculum units in photoplay appreciation based on the showing of feature film excerpts or complete photoplays in classrooms and auditoriums. In this way, the schools can do something about the problem of improving movie habits. Why not form a committee in your own school to consider the matter? The National Council of Teachers of English can help you.

Developing good taste in the selection of motion pictures depends on many factors which have been described in this book. Not the least of these is the exchange of opinions about films that you have seen. To discuss a common experience with someone is a good way to check your own ideas and reactions. It is surprising how often we find that other persons have had very much the same reaction that we have. When another person differs with us, we have a chance to gain new ideas and points of view. Talking about recent movies provides a good basis for becoming acquainted with other young persons, at school and elsewhere.

There are many ways to become a good movie-goer, but the main requirement is that one be alert to learn as much as possible about what makes movies good or bad and that he use each experience in selecting a motion picture as an exercise in discrimination. The more good films we see, the better able we are to distinguish superior movies from those that are poor ones.

Motion pictures will inevitably become just as good as we *want* them to become. The customer decides the quality of the product.

Suggested Activities

1. In surveying the magazines listed in this chapter, decide which carry the best film reviews as far as you are concerned. Discuss the reasons for your choice.

2. If you have studied this book early in the term, follow up your study by keeping track of reviews of current movies and posting critical opinions on a portion of the classroom bulletin board reserved for that purpose.

3. If you live in a large city, investigate the differences among motion-picture theaters as to the kinds of pictures they show. Do you have any theaters that feature films made for selected audiences? Are there colleges or museums or film societies in your community that sponsor the showing of noteworthy films? Report your findings to the class.

4. What films are available on television? How can you

find out beforehand which films are to be shown? Check the films to be shown against lists of award-winning films provided in this book. Try to see films that have contributed something to the development of the motion picture.

5. Keep a card file on the movies you see. In addition to the name of the film and the date on which you saw it, record the names of the leading actors, the director, the producer, and others whose work may interest you. Also summarize briefly the story of the film and your general reaction to it. Building such a card file will do much to broaden your knowledge of the outstanding persons in the film industry and will provide you with an increasingly better basis of judging whether a new motion picture is probably worth going to see.

16

What Shall We Read About the Movies?

To BECOME well-informed about films you ought to read books about them. Following is a list of nine books which may be found in most public libraries and in some school libraries. Make yourself a more intelligent movie-goer by perusing several of these publications. Come prepared to report to your class on the one you liked best. If you prefer, you may report your reactions to any five critical reviews of current films in newspapers and magazines or on three recent issues of *Photoplay Studies*.

1. FILM DAILY YEAR BOOK OF MOTION PICTURES. Jack Alicoate, Editor. The Film Daily, 1501 Broadway, New York 18. $5.00. Published annually since 1918.

The oldest encyclopedia of filmdom. Universally recognized as a standard book of reference concerning the multifarious activities of the motion-picture industry.

2. THE GREAT AUDIENCE. By Gilbert Seldes, 299 pp. The Viking Press, 18 East 48th St., New York 17. 1950. $3.75.

A searching, critical analysis of the movies, radio, and

television as mass media of entertainment. Written by an expert, in lively style.

3. HOLLYWOOD LOOKS AT ITS AUDIENCE. By Leo A. Handel. Foreword by Paul S. Lazarsfeld. 240 pp. University of Illinois Press, Urbana, Ill. 1950. $3.50.

An illuminating report of procedures and findings of film audience research, with detailed explanations of techniques for analyzing public habits and attitudes in relation to movies and particular elements of movies.

4. HOLLYWOOD, U.S.A. By Alice Evans Field. Introduction by Will Hays. 256 pp. Illustrated. Vantage Press, Inc., 231 West 41st St., New York 18. 1952. $3.50.

A public-relations representative of the motion-picture industry takes us on a popular tour of the studios and explains the "assembly line," from script to screen, in light, readable style.

5. IDEAS ON FILM. Edited by Cecile Starr. Foreword by Irving Jacoby. 251 pp. Funk & Wagnalls Co., 153 East 24th St., New York 10. 1951. $4.50.

The editor of the documentary film department of the *Saturday Review* presents a splendid collection of 29 articles on documentary and educational films by 20 experts, including a number of excellent articles by herself and 200 reviews of short films. Most of the material is reprinted from *SR*.

6. MOTION-PICTURE AND TELEVISION ALMANAC. Edited by Charles S. Aaronson. Quigley Publishing Co., 1270 Sixth Ave., New York 20. $5.00. Published annually since 1928.

Nearly half of this 1000-page tome is devoted to a *Who's Who in Motion Pictures and Television,* including more than

12,000 biographies. This is followed by an annual survey of film facts.

7. MOTION PICTURES. By Samuel Beckoff. 113 pp. Oxford Book Co., 227 Fourth Ave., New York 3. 1953. 40¢.

One of an excellently-written series of pamphlets on the communication arts.

8. NOT BY A LONG SHOT. By Margaret Cussler. 200 pp. Illustrated. Exposition Press, 386 Fourth Ave., New York 16. 1951. $3.00.

An informative account of the adventures of two young women in making 16mm documentary sound films in various parts of the U.S.A.

9. THE RISE OF THE AMERICAN FILM. By Lewis Jacobs. Preface by Iris Barry. 585 pp. Illustrated. Harcourt, Brace and Co., 383 Madison Ave., New York 17. Revised edition. 1948. $6.00.

The best history of American films in print and the first critical account of the movie in America in its commercial, artistic, and social aspects.

17

Glossary of Motion-Picture Terms

THE ACADEMY of Motion Picture Arts and Sciences, 9038 Melrose Avenue, Hollywood, California, has published *A Selected Glossary for the Motion-Picture Technican*. A list of definitions has been published also by the Society of Motion Picture Engineers, Hotel Statler, 33rd Street and Seventh Avenue, New York City. Here are some simplified definitions for students. Try to find illustrations of these items, with a view to contributing to a class project for compiling a pictorial movie dictionary.

Boom: Long steel structure holding a camera, with seats for the cameraman and director, which can be raised, lowered, or swung in a circle from a heavy base on wheels, to follow the action of a scene with complete mobility.
Camera angle: Viewpoint from which a scene is photographed.
Cinematography: Motion-picture photography.
Close-up: Photographic shot made with the camera close to to an object or person.
Continuity: Continuous development of action.
Cutter: Editor who selects and arranges the shots which make up the scenes of a film.

Dissolve: Gradual transition from one photographed scene to another by overlapping.

Documentary: A non-fiction, factual, poetical, or propaganda film; one with educational or special artistic value, rather than general entertainment or amusement value.

Dolly: Rolling platform, often large enough to carry camera, cameraman, and director.

Exterior: Scene showing action out-of-doors, even if photographed on a stage; as against interior, scene supposed to be photographed inside a building.

Extra: An actor employed by the day for scenes of group or mass action.

Fade-in: Gradual appearance of a scene from darkness to brilliance.

Fade-out: Gradual disappearance of a bright scene into blackness, the opposite of fade-in.

Feature: Full-length film running usually about 90 minutes.

Flashback: A scene in which the action reverts to previous events in order to reveal background action necessary to an understanding of character or plot.

Focus: Adjustment of lens to secure a sharp image.

Footage: Length of film in feet.

Frame: Single picture on film. (Movies are usually photographed at the rate of 24 frames per second.)

Glass-shot: Shot taken partly by means of a transparent effect on a sheet of glass placed in front of the camera to coincide in perspective with a constructed set.

Grip: Skilled laborer, usually a carpenter, who can make quick changes of settings during production.

Heavy: Villain or unsympathetic character.

Iris in: To adjust a diaphragm on a lens so as to reveal a scene in a gradually widening circle.

Iris out: Opposite of iris in.

Key scene: One of the main scenes in the continuity of a film.

Lap dissolve: Duplicate exposure or overlapping scenes, for transitional purposes.

Lip-sync: Coordination or synchonization of the movement of an actor's lips with the sound of his voice.

Long shot: View photographed from a distance.

Montage: "Mounting" or assembling of a series of brief shots which may be unrelated but which build a dramatic effect.

Pan: To swing the camera for a panoramic shot—sideways, upward, or downward, from a fixed position, as a person would move his head.

Parallel action: Alternation of scenes made in different locations but intercut so as to go back and forth rapidly, revealing what is going on in two places at the same time.

Prop: Any movable object needed in a scene, such as a piece of furniture, a weapon, or a household article.

Scenario: Complete screenplay, including full descriptions of characters, action, continuity, and dialog, scene by scene and shot by shot; sometimes called "shooting script," because this is what the director uses when shooting scenes.

Scene: Unit of action, often composed of several shots.

Set: Interior or exterior background, built under the supervision of an art director or architect.

Shot: Photograph made from a single camera position, often a small portion of the scene.

Spotlight: Powerful incandescent lamp for throwing illumination where needed.

Still: Glossy photograph, usually 8 x 10 inches, made by a still cameraman on a movie set and used for publicity.

18

A Photoplay Approach to Shakespeare

John Gielgud as Cassius and James Mason as Brutus in the M-G-M screen version of Shakespeare's *Julius Caesar,* now available to schools in 16mm through Films Incorporated, a subsidiary of Encyclopaedia Britannica Films, Wilmette, Illinois.

A Guide to the Discussion of the Metro-Goldwyn-Mayer Screen Version of William Shakespeare's
JULIUS CAESAR

PREPARED BY WILLIAM LEWIN, PH.D., Editor of *Photoplay Studies*

Why is Shakespeare's great historical tragedy *Julius Caesar*, written 350 years ago, about events that took place 2,000 years ago, timely today?

It is timely because it concerns dictatorship, conspiracy, assassination, demagoguery, rabble-rousing, and civil war—problems with which the world is concerned today.

Julius Caesar

Julius Caesar, born in 100 B.C. and assassinated in 44 B.C., was a truly great Roman. To motivate the action of the group of men who formed a conspiracy to murder him, Caesar appears in the play as rather overbearing, imperious, and boastful, lacking the virtues of modesty, kindness, and generosity which he really possessed. Bernard Shaw, who criticized Shakespeare's characterization of Caesar as absurd, tried to show the real Caesar in his own play, *Caesar and Cleopatra*. It is only fair to say that Shakespeare's portrayal of Caesar as arrogant is not true to history. However, Shakespeare's characterizations of Brutus, Cassius, and Antony are so true and brilliant that they compensate for the inaccuracies in the characterization of Caesar. It might be said that Shakespeare shows Caesar as the conspirators saw him, rather than as he was.

Actually Caesar was no tyrant. He was sincerely devoted

to the public interest—generous, forgiving, magnanimous, democratic. He went about unarmed and unguarded, mingling freely with the Roman people, whom he loved and with whom he was extremely popular. Caesar showed great genius in war and peace—conquering and uniting all of Europe, reforming the vast Roman government, and planning great improvements. The Roman Senate, having great confidence in him, appointed him dictator for life.

The Conspiracy

But not all the leading Romans approved of Caesar's dictatorship. At the time when Shakespeare's play opens, violent political storm-clouds were gathering. Many liberty-loving, artistocratic Romans were so strongly opposed to the idea of dictatorship that they preferred death to slavish obedience to an absolute ruler. Thus it was that a group of conspirators, headed by Marcus Brutus and his brother-in-law, Caius Cassius, determined to assassinate Caesar. Had they not tragically underestimated the skill of Mark Antony, Caesar's close political associate, the plotters might have won control of Rome and its far-flung dominions.

Marcus Brutus

The tragic hero of Shakespeare's play is really Brutus. He was a true patriot, who, though he loved Caesar personally as a dear friend, was willing to sacrifice his friend's life, and even his own life, for the good of his country. Fifteen years younger than Caesar, Brutus survived Caesar by only two years, committing suicide at the age of 43, when defeated in battle by Antony and Octavius Caesar.

Brutus's enemies respected him so much that Antony acknowledged in the end that Brutus was "the noblest Roman of them all"; that he was honestly devoted to the common good; that though he had murdered Caesar, "his life was gentle"; and that "Nature might stand up and say to all the world, 'This was a man!' " Brutus exemplifies the old motto of the Romans that it is "sweet to die for one's country."

What makes Brutus's character, then, so tragic? Like most of Shakespeare's other tragic heroes, Brutus had a fatal defect in his personality. In Hamlet the fatal flaw was indecision; in Romeo it was a hasty, impulsive nature; in Macbeth it was "vaulting ambition that o'erleaps itself"; in Brutus it was *impracticality*. Brutus was "arm'd so strong in honesty," so completely devoted to ideals of honor, justice, and self-sacrifice, that *he failed to see the practical side of politics*. Though others in the conspiracy felt it would be advisable to have Antony and Caesar fall together, Brutus insisted, for humanitarian reasons, that Antony be spared and even that Antony be allowed to speak at Caesar's funeral.

Shakespeare was so much interested in the complex character of Brutus that he made him the central figure of his play and constructed his drama in terms of the rise and fall of the fortunes of Brutus. He assigned the part of Brutus to the star player of his Globe Theater stock company, Richard Burbage, the actor who first spoke the great lines of Romeo, Hamlet, Macbeth, Richard III, Henry V, and other great Shakespearean characters.

Caius Cassius

It was Cassius who persuaded his patriotic and respected brother-in-law, Brutus, to lead the plotters. Cassius had been a general in the Roman army, had fought on the side of Pompey against Caesar, had been defeated by Caesar, in the battle of Pharsalus, in Greece, four years before the play opens, had been pardoned by Caesar and been made a Roman judge.

Cassius still hated his former foe. Even though Caesar had refused a crown, Cassius suspected that Caesar still intended to make himself a king and thus bring to an end the old heritage of freedom which Romans had enjoyed for nearly five centuries.

Though Caesar had personally been quite generous to Cassius, as indeed Caesar had been to all his former foes, Cassius was so proud and aristocratic, so intensely concerned with individual liberty, that he could not brook even the idea of dictatorship.

What do the lines spoken by Cassius, as he whets Brutus against Caesar, signify today? They mean that in ancient Rome and in the modern world—though 2,000 years may lie between—the price of freedom is eternal vigilance.

Mark Antony

Though Caesar is the most famous character in the play and gives the play its title; though Brutus is the central figure, the tragic hero; and though Cassius is the mainspring which sets the plot in motion, it is Antony who is the play's most exciting figure in the M-G-M production.

Antony was at the height of his mental, moral, and physical powers when Caesar was struck down. Seventeen years younger than Caesar, Antony was still a handsome athlete. He had a quick, shrewd, and brilliant mind. His famous oration over the body of Caesar is one of the greatest passages in Shakespeare. It marks the turning point in the drama.

Antony is the leading character in another of Shakespeare's

Director Joseph Mankiewicz explains to Marlon Brando an effect needed in the forum scene of *Julius Caesar*.

tragedies, *Antony and Cleopatra,* which constitutes a sequel to *Julius Caesar* and describes Antony's downfall. In that play we find Antony neglecting his duties as one of the rulers of Rome, falling under the spell of Egypt's beautiful queen, and dying on his own sword after his defeat by his brother-in-law and former comrade-in-arms, Octavius Caesar, who in turn is destined to become the first Roman emperor, with the title Augustus.

Portia and Calpurnia

There are only two women in the play: Portia, Brutus's devoted wife, and Calpurnia, Caesar's wife, who feared for his safety. The parts played by these women are small, yet they serve significantly to develop the characters of Brutus and Caesar. Deborah Kerr's fine performance as Portia reveals Shakespeare's purpose of having Brutus's wife place him on a pedestal of devotion by kneeling before him, begging him to reveal the secret problems that disturb his sleep. She wins from Brutus a touching expression of loving-kindness.

Portia's entreaties serve to build audience respect for Brutus, supplementing Casca's lines when he lauds Brutus and those of Cassius when he bows to Brutus as the leader of the conspiracy, even though he realizes that Brutus is making serious political mistakes.

Calpurnia elicits from Caesar his famous dictum that "cowards die many times before their deaths; the valiant never taste of death but once." Calpurnia also serves to build suspense on the morning of the ides of March. Will she keep Caesar at home? How are the conspirators to bring him to the Capitol? Perhaps their plans will go awry because of Calpurnia's fears for Caesar's life.

Historical Sources

Shakespeare obtained his information mainly from a collection of biographies entitled *Parallel Lives of Noble Greeks and Romans,* written by a Greek writer named Plutarch who lived about 100 years after the time of Julius Caesar. These excellent character studies, 46 in all, were newly translated into English in Shakespeare's time by Sir Thomas North, and Shakespeare found them to be treasure-troves of dramatic material. Included in the series are accounts of the lives of Caesar, Brutus, and Antony, each about 50 pages in length.

There is a one-volume edition of *Plutarch's Lives* in the series of Modern Library "Giants," based on John Dryden's translation, as revised and modernized by Arthur H. Clough.

The M-G-M Production

The chief problem in making a popular screen production of a Shakespearean play is to make the language of 350 years ago intelligible to audiences of the English-speaking world today. To solve this problem, producer John Houseman and director Joseph Mankiewicz assembled a cast of players who excelled in clarity of diction. The lines of Shakespearean poetry are delivered effectively by the extraordinary assemblage of performers—Marlon Brando, James Mason, John Gielgud, Louis Calhern, Deborah Kerr, Greer Garson—each a star of the first magnitude. Director Mankiewicz was able to coordinate the performances of these powerful personalities to good effect. Producer Houseman's job was to "orchestrate" the diverse minds and elements of the production so as to secure a smooth, harmonious result.

Suggested Activities

1. Bring in a report on highlights of Roman history, based on encyclopedia articles or on books in your local library.
2. Come prepared to mention highlights in the life of Julius Caesar, including some of his adventures, conquests, decisions, and plans for reforms.
3. Contrast the character traits of Brutus and Cassius.
4. How would you describe Antony? Did you enjoy Marlon Brando's delivery of the famous oration?

5. How does the play exemplify rabble-rousing? Do mobs today behave as they did in Caesar's time?

6. Mention three minor differences between the stage-play and the photoplay—something added, something omitted, and something changed. Would you say that the film follows the play closely?

7. Does the M-G-M screen version of *Julius Caesar* help you to understand any scenes of the play that were previously unclear to you?

8. What scenes in the photoplay version did you find most impressive? Did any scenes bore you?

9. Did you feel that the actors were speaking poetical lines? Was the language clear and natural, on the whole, or did it seem artificial? To what extent was it beyond your comprehension?

10. Discuss the timeliness and social significance of *Julius Caesar*.

Suggested Follow-up Readings

> *Shakespeare as a Playwright,* by Brander Matthews.
> *The Elizabethan People,* by H. T. Stephenson.
> *Master Skylark,* by John Bennett.
> *Kenilworth,* by Walter Scott.
> *Shakespeare's Christmas,* by A. T. Quiller-Couch.
> Plutarch's *Lives* of Caesar, Brutus, and Antony.
> *A Friend of Caesar,* by William Stearns Davis.
> *A Day in Old Rome,* by William Stearns Davis.
> *Caesar,* by F. W. Fowler.
> *The Book of Ancient Romans,* by Dorothy Mills.
> *Two Thousand Years Ago,* by A. J. Church.
> *With Caesar's Legions,* by R. F. Wells.

Synopsis of the Photoplay

The play begins on the pagan feast day of Lupercal. Roman citizens in holiday attire, on their way to athletic games in the stadium, pause to decorate the dictator's statues with flowers and laurel wreaths. Two Tribunes tear the floral offerings down and urge the crowds to disperse, reminding them of past celebrations in Pompey's honor. The Tribunes are arrested promptly for interfering with the celebration.

En route to the stadium with his entourage, Julius Caesar is hailed in the street by a Soothsayer, who cries out, "Beware the ides of March." Ignoring the warning, Caesar proceeds.

As the remainder of the throng enters the stadium, Cassius, leader of the intrigue against Caesar, catches the eye of Brutus and engages him in conversation. Playing on the other's high-mindedness and pride, Cassius tries to enlist Brutus in the conspiracy against Caesar, knowing that Brutus's reputation for fairness and honesty will give the enterprise prestige and respectability in the eyes of the Roman public.

Three great cheers are heard, at intervals, from inside the stadium. Their meaning is explained to Brutus and Cassius a few minutes later by surly Casca. During the games Caesar's political associate, Mark Antony, has three times offered Caesar a king's crown—and Caesar, apparently with increasing reluctance, has three times refused it.

Partially convinced that Caesar's blood must be the price of the Republic's freedom, Brutus goes home. Cassius arranges for letters supposedly written by Roman citizens, urging Brutus to "strike" and "redress" the wrongs of dictatorship, to be placed where Brutus will find them.

The conspirators plan to strike their fatal blow against Caesar on the ides of March. That night Rome's sleep is disturbed by a violent storm of wind, thunder, and lightning.

In the storm's pre-dawn waning, Cassius, Casca, and the other conspirators come to the garden of Brutus's house to complete the details of their plot. Brutus agrees that Caesar must be assassinated but vetoes the proposal that Mark Antony also be killed.

When the conspirators leave, his wife Portia finds Brutus in the garden and begs him to tell her the secret which troubles him. Brutus is at first evasive, and then promises to tell her everything "by and by."

The stormy night has also disturbed the slumbers of Caesar's wife Calpurnia. She has had a most terrifying dream of Caesar's murder and implores him not to go to the Senate that day. One of the conspirators who arrives in the morning as a member of the Dictator's escort to the Senate, however, craftily interprets Calpurnia's dream as a favorable omen. Caesar decides to go to the Senate, where he is led to believe the formal offer of a crown awaits him.

At the Capitol Caesar fails to heed a second warning of the Soothsayer's that the ides of March are not yet past. He leaves unopened a message in which a friend reveals names of the men plotting against him.

Then, with Mark Antony drawn away according to their prearranged plan, the conspirators crowd around Caesar to urge a hopeless petition for the pardon of an exiled Roman. When Caesar refuses, first Casca, then the other conspirators, and finally Brutus, stab him to death.

Antony, feigning willingness to collaborate with the assassins, obtains permission from Brutus to speak at Caesar's funeral.

The Roman street crowd which gathers for the funeral, moved by Brutus's oratory, at first accepts the explanation that Caesar's death was their only safeguard against his ambition.

Then Mark Antony mounts the platform. With several ironic references to Brutus as "an honorable man," Antony eloquently and shrewdly fans his listeners' passions until the crowd becomes a violent mob crying vows of vengeance against Caesar's assassins.

The conspirators flee the city, leaving Rome under control of Mark Antony and Octavius Caesar, who conduct a ruthless purge of suspected political enemies.

Civil war ensues, in which the alliance between Brutus and Cassius is strained by personal differences. At their military camp in Macedonia the two leaders quarrel violently over Cassius's "itching palm" and "corruption" in taxation and filling public offices. They eventually are reconciled and Brutus reveals he has been under a strain following news of the suicide of Portia.

Cassius yields to Brutus on a vital point of strategy, against his own better military judgment, and they agree to meet the enemy on the Plains of Philippi. The night before the battle Brutus sees the apparition of Caesar in his tent. The ghost tells him they will meet at Philippi.

Troops under command of Cassius are defeated in the battle by those of Antony. Cassius hands his sword to a slave and orders the slave to kill him. The slave obeys, and Cassius dies from a thrust of the same weapon he raised against Caesar.

The second front of battle is turned against Brutus by Octavius. Hopelessly defeated, Brutus pleads with his friends to slay him before they flee the field. When they refuse, he places his sword in the hand of a faithful servant and tells the servant to turn his face away. Brutus falls upon his sword and dies.

Later, Antony, standing above the body of Brutus in the latter's tent, speaks this tribute:

This was the noblest Roman of them all:
All the conspirators, save only he,
Did that they did in envy of great Caesar;
He only, in a general honest thought
And common good to all, made one of them.
His life was gentle, and the elements
So mix'd in him that Nature might stand up
And say to all the world, "This was a man!"

Chief Members of the Cast in Order of Appearance

Louis Calhern	Julius Caesar
Edmond O'Brien	Casca
Greer Garson	Calpurnia
Deborah Kerr	Portia
Marlon Brando	Mark Antony
James Mason	Brutus
John Gielgud	Cassius
William Cottrell	Cinna
John Hoyt	Decius Brutus
Tom Powers	Metellus Cimber
Jack Raine	Trebonius
Ian Wolfe	Ligarius
Lumsden Hare	Publius
Douglas Watson	Octavius Caesar
Douglass Dumbrille	Lepidus

Two filmstrips (97 lighted pictures for projection), presenting a complete pictorial guide to the M-G-M screen version of *Julius Caesar* (Part 1, 55 frames; Part 2, 42 frames), are available through Educational & Recreational Guides, Inc., 10 Brainerd Road, Summit, New Jersey, at $6.00 a set.

A Photoplay Approach to Shakespeare • 135

1. Two Tribunes scold the crowd for rejoicing over Caesar's growing power.

2. A Soothsayer bids Caesar, on his way to the stadium, to beware the ides of March.

3. Brutus and Cassius look with concern at Caesar's extraordinary power.

4. Returning from the stadium, Caesar confides to Antony that he dislikes Cassius.

A Photoplay Approach to Shakespeare • 137

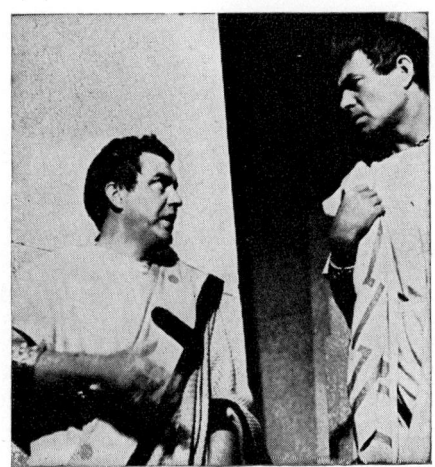

5. Casca reports that Antony, at the stadium, thrice offered Caesar a crown.

6. Before long, Casca joins Cassius in his conspiracy to assassinate Caesar.

7. After long meditation, Brutus decides to join the conspiracy against Caesar.

8. Dominating the group, Brutus insists that Antony be spared. This proves a fatal error.

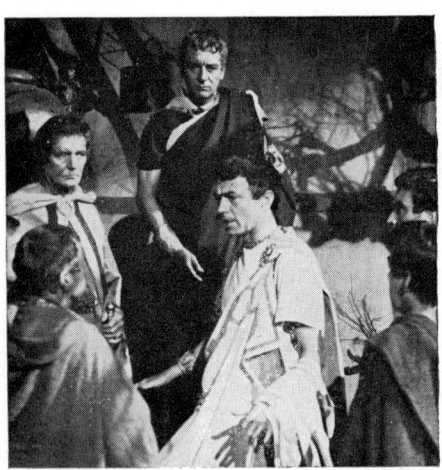

A Photoplay Approach to Shakespeare • 139

9. Portia, Brutus's wife, is greatly worried over her husband's mysterious visitors.

10. While Portia worries over Brutus, Calpurnia begs Caesar not to go to the Capitol.

11. Caesar says he is not afraid to die, but, to please his wife, agrees to stay home.

12. Decius, in spite of Calpurnia, persuades Caesar to come to the Capitol.

A Photoplay Approach to Shakespeare • 141

13. On the way to the Capitol, Artemidorus tries unsuccessfully to warn Caesar.

14. The suspense mounts as Brutus and Cassius fear they are discovered.

15. Cassius tells Brutus he will slay himself if the plot is discovered.

16. Caesar takes his chair and asks what business is before the Roman Senate.

17. The conspirators' plan is to surround Caesar, as if asking for a favor.

18. Casca rears his hand as the signal for assassination: "Speak, hands, for me!"

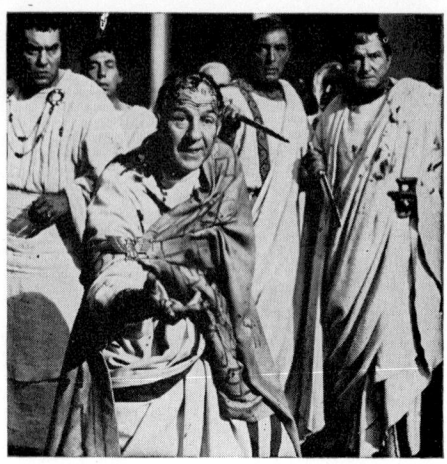

19. Bleeding, Caesar looks hopefully to his friend Brutus for help.

20. But whichever way Caesar turns, he sees daggers pointed at him.

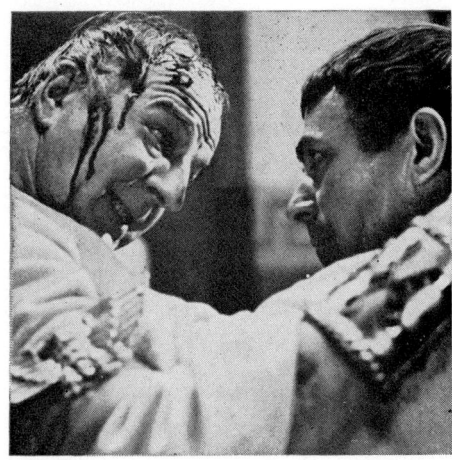

21. "Et tu, Brute!" ("And you, Brutus!"), cries Caesar as Brutus stabs.

22. The conspirators ceremoniously bathe their hands in Caesar's blood.

23. Antony shrewdly asks the conspirators for permission to speak at Caesar's funeral.

24. Though Brutus consents to let Antony speak, Cassius has grave misgivings.

A Photoplay Approach to Shakespeare • 147

25. In a famous soliloquy Antony vows to "let slip the dogs of war" against the conspirators.

26. Brutus explains to the mob that Caesar was murdered to save the Republic.

27. "I have the same dagger for myself when it shall please my country to need my death."

28. Antony, introduced by Brutus, carries Caesar's body to the forum.

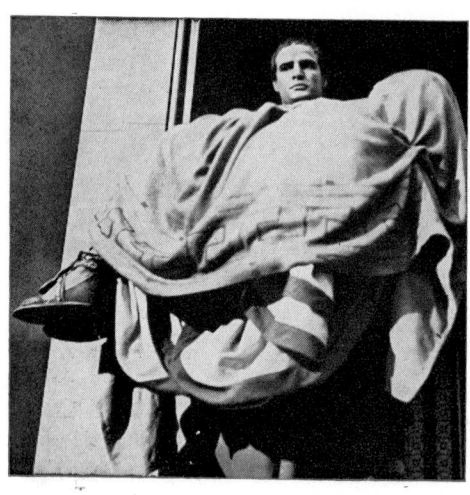

29. This opportunity to address the mob is all that Antony needs.

30. Antony begins his famous oration with humble words.

31. "I thrice presented him a kingly crown, Which he did thrice refuse; was this ambition?"

32. Antony ironically keeps repeating that the conspirators are "honorable men."

33. Antony reveals that Caesar's will bequeaths money to every Roman citizen.

34. The effect is to rouse the mob to a frenzy against the plotters.

35. He says that if he were an orator like Brutus, he'd start a mutiny.

36. "Pluck down forms, windows, anything." The mob seeks revenge.

A Photoplay Approach to Shakespeare • 153

37. Octavius and Lepidus join Antony to take over the government.

38. Pursued to Macedonia, Brutus and Cassius encamp with their armies.

39. Two years after Caesar's death, Brutus awaits a decisive battle.

40. Brutus, always an impractical idealist, and Cassius, a practical man, quarrel.

A Photoplay Approach to Shakespeare • 155

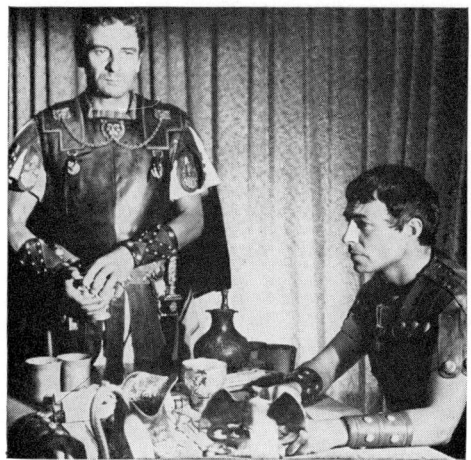

41. Settling their quarrel, the conspirators plan to attack Antony and Octavius.

42. Brutus sees a specter in his tent, looking like Caesar's ghost: "I will see thee at Philippi."

43. Antony gives the signal for battle at Philippi.

44. Antony's soldiers shower the conspirators' forces with arrows.

A Photoplay Approach to Shakespeare • 157

45. The army of Cassius suffers a serious setback.

46. Antony leads his cavalry to victory over Brutus and Cassius.

47. The conspirators are surrounded.

48. Brutus's best men are killed.

A Photoplay Approach to Shakespeare

49. Hope gone, Cassius orders his servant to stab him with the sword that stabbed Caesar.

50. Brutus runs on his sword, rather than be brought to Rome as a captive.

160 • Standards of Photoplay Appreciation

51. "Caesar, now be still; I killed not thee with half so good a will."

REPRINTS of this illustrated guide to the M-G-M screen version of *Julius Caesar* are available in small quantities at fifty cents a copy, or in 100 lots at thirty cents a copy, from Educational & Recreational Guides, Inc., 10 Brainerd Road, Summit, New Jersey. The guide is one of a series called *Photoplay Studies,* published regularly since 1935. Subscription price: $3 a year, $5 for two years.

PHOTOPLAY FILMSTRIPS may also be ordered at $7.50 each at the same address. These are in color and are based on the following photoplays: *Knights of the Round Table, Ulysses, Richard III, Robinson Crusoe, Romeo and Juliet, The Glass Slipper, Hansel and Gretel, The Greatest Show on Earth,* and *Alexander the Great.* The filmstrips and *Photoplay Studies* constitute a "kit of tools" to aid in introducing the study of photoplay appreciation.